# Inclusive Songs *from the* Heart of Gospel

Jann Aldredge-Clanton
with McKenzie Brown and Larry E. Schultz

All rights reserved. With the purchase of 10 or more copies of this book, unlimited permission to reproduce and broadcast the songs is given. Otherwise, please contact ONE LICENSE for the reprinting and broadcasting of these hymns (onelicense.net). Copyright information must be included at the bottom of any reproduced song along with this phrase: From *Inclusive Songs from the Heart of Gospel* (Eakin Press, 2022).

Copyright © 2022
By Jann Aldredge-Clanton
Published By Eakin Press
An Imprint of Wild Horse Media Group
P.O. Box 331779
Fort Worth, Texas 76163
1-817-344-7036
**www.EakinPress.com**
**ALL RIGHTS RESERVED**
1 2 3 4 5 6 7 8 9
Paperback ISBN 978-1-68179-297-2
Hardback ISBN 978-1-68179-298-9
eBook ISBN 978-1-68179-299-6

# CONTENTS

Introduction .................................................................................................. 5

Songs (Numbers 1–74) ............................................................................... 19

Notes on the Songs ................................................................................... 117

Indexes

    Topical Index of Songs ....................................................................... 129

    Index of Scripture References ............................................................ 158

    Index of Composers, Authors, and Sources .................................... 160

    Alphabetical Index of Tunes ............................................................. 162

    Metrical Index of Tunes ..................................................................... 164

    Index of Titles ..................................................................................... 167

# INTRODUCTION

The title of this new collection, *Inclusive Songs from the Heart of Gospel*, comes from our choice of gospel tunes for the majority of our texts. This title is likewise appropriate for our songs set to other familiar hymn tunes because we draw from the meaning of the Greek New Testament word for "gospel," *euangelion*, also translated as "good news." We reclaim these gospel tunes and other tunes we love with inclusive lyrics to proclaim the good news of liberation, justice, peace, equity, and abundant life.

## Creative Collaboration

For this new song collection, I collaborated for the first time with McKenzie Brown, an emerging lyricist and composer. She wrote lyrics for some of the songs in this collection, collaborated with me in writing lyrics on several other songs, gave me valuable critique on many of my songs, and contributed to the creation of the title.

McKenzie majored in religion at Texas Wesleyan University. She was a top student of her religion professor and faculty advisor, Kendra Weddle, my friend and co-author of *Building Bridges: Letha Dawson Scanzoni and Friends*.[1] McKenzie's undergraduate program included a semester at Oxford, where she focused on feminist philosophy of religion. After she graduated from Texas Wesleyan, she continued to study feminist philosophy. At an annual conference of the Southwest Commission on Religious Studies, she presented a paper using feminist philosophy to analyze the problem of evil. During her undergraduate days and after, McKenzie also pursued her love of music, composing and playing songs on her guitar.

From the fall of 2018 through 2019, McKenzie and I met often at Freebirds World Burrito Mexican Restaurant to talk about our songs. We found a quiet spot, and, over our burrito bowls, we often sang to each other new songs we had drafted and brought for feedback. Not only did we review our songs, but we also discussed our process of writing and our reasons for writing lyrics. McKenzie stirred me to reflect more deeply on my philosophy of hymn writing.

When she was a student at Texas Wesleyan, I had first connected with McKenzie at the 2014 Christian Feminism Today Gathering in St. Louis, where she gave a presentation. I was impressed by the depth of her presentation titled "Disingenuous Hermeneutic: The Relationship Between Biblical Interpretation and the Marginalization of Female Leaders." She came to a workshop I presented, "Inclusive Music for All Ages." Afterward, she stayed to talk about her passion for inclusivity in worship language as well as in leadership. She told me that she especially appreciated the divine female names and images included in my songs in the workshop, and that a highlight of the Gathering for her was the inclusive language used throughout the meeting. For the first time she had experienced female divine names and images in story, song, prayers, and scholarly presentations.

Near the beginning of our collaboration on this collection, McKenzie wrote "We Are Rising Up Together" to the tune UNBROKEN CIRCLE. In this song she expresses her delight in finding community in Christian Feminism Today, beginning with these stanzas:

*I was standing, with convictions*
*but alone from day to day.*
*And I wondered, were there others*
*who could help me find my way?*

*Then one day I found my people,*
*for the first time, unconstrained.*
*We rejoiced and started planning*
*how to ease the world of pain.*

McKenzie sang "We Are Rising Up Together" at the national Nevertheless She Preached 2018 Conference, and it has become a favorite of New Wineskins Community in Dallas, Texas.

For *Inclusive Songs from the Heart of Gospel*, I also collaborated with composer Larry E. Schultz. He wrote fresh arrangements of traditional tunes for some of the songs in this collection. He also created lyrics and music for some new songs. Larry and I have previously collaborated on *Inclusive Hymns for Liberating Christians*; *Inclusive Hymns for Liberation, Peace, and Justice*; *Earth Transformed with Music! Inclusive Songs for Worship*; *Inclusive Songs for Resistance & Social Action*;[2] *Imagine God! A Children's Musical Exploring and Expressing Images of God*;[3] *Sing and Dance and Play with Joy! Inclusive Songs for Young Children*;[4] and choral anthems.[5]

## Reclaiming and Reimagining the Gospel

A little while after we began writing lyrics for this new collection, John Ballenger invited me to co-lead with him a workshop at the annual Alliance of Baptists Gathering, scheduled for April 23-26, 2020. The theme of the Gathering was reimagining atonement theology from a progressive Christian viewpoint. The topic of our workshop was hymnody and liturgy on the theme of atonement for progressive churches. John's invitation came in April of 2019, and we began planning our workshop in May and were moving forward with our plans in January of 2020.

In March of 2020, near the beginning of the coronavirus pandemic, the Alliance leaders followed medical safety guidelines and made the wise decision to cancel the Gathering. They contacted presenters to let us know that a progressive view of atonement would be the theme of a future Gathering, and that we would then have the opportunity to lead our workshop.

When John invited me to co-lead a workshop and told me the Gathering theme, my initial reaction was hesitance about leading a workshop or even attending a Gathering on a theme of atonement. I was thinking about the substitutionary theory of atonement that has prevailed in Christianity, prominent in my worship experience growing up in a Southern Baptist church, no longer good news to me. This substitutionary atonement theology teaches that Jesus had to die in our place to reconcile sinful humanity to God. In my mind the word "atonement" was associated with blood and sacrifice. I grew up singing what some Christians have called the "bloody" hymns because the words emphasize blood redemption.

As I considered John's invitation, I started looking back at some other classic atonement theories I had studied in seminary and wondering what the atonement would look like from feminist and womanist viewpoints. Then I found several analyses of the *Christus Victor* theory as helpful for marginalized and oppressed groups in that it envisions the overcoming of all injustice, and of the moral influence theory as viewing Jesus as an example of suffering for resisting unjust systems and bringing justice, peace, and love to humanity. Womanist theologian Kelly Brown Douglas views the crucifixion as the result of Jesus's challenging hegemonic, oppressive power structures, and states "that God responded to the crucifixion not with approval of this evil attack on the human body, but with the resurrection," an affirmation of life.[6] For feminist theologian Elizabeth Johnson, the cross is "the parable that enacts Sophia-God's participation in the suffering of the world."[7] Womanist theologian Dolores Williams also challenges the substitutionary theory of atonement, raising the question of whether this view has salvific power for Black women or whether the image of a surrogate-God "supports and reinforces the exploitation that has accompanied their experience with surrogacy."[8]

Also, I remembered that I had recently written lyrics to some gospel tunes for this collaborative collection. The original words of many gospel hymns, based on substitutionary atonement theology, glorify violence and death rather than the abundant life Jesus taught (John 10:10). In some of these hymns, there is incongruity between text and tune; for example, "There Is Power in the Blood" is set to a rousing tune. I reclaimed this upbeat tune with a text that celebrates "Power in Us All," beginning with this stanza:

*Wisdom within us is boundless and free;*
*there's power in us all, power in us all;*
*She moves us forward to all we can be;*
*there's life-giving power in us all.*

When I looked at these lyrics and others I had written to gospel tunes with "bloody" original texts, I accepted John's invitation to co-lead the Alliance workshop. I continued to write lyrics reimagining atonement theology and setting them to these tunes. "Are You Washed in the Blood?" and "There Is a Fountain Filled with Blood" gave me nightmares when I was a child, so it was healing for me to write new lyrics to the familiar tunes of these hymns. My song "So Many People Cry in Pain," to the tune CLEANSING FOUNTAIN, affirms the power of Wisdom's peace and love to bring rebirth, concluding with this stanza:

*She keeps on calling out for peace,*
*though often mocked and scorned;*
*Her loving power will still increase,*
*and all will be reborn,*
*and all will be reborn,*
*and all will be reborn.*
*Her loving power will still increase,*
*and all will be reborn.*

My commitment to including female divine names and images in hymns led me to wonder how they would fit in others of my favorite gospel hymn tunes, such as OLD RUGGED CROSS. I found that the Female Divine provided a counterpoint to the familiar substitutionary atonement words and enhanced reimagining a theology centering peace, love, and life. I reclaimed the OLD RUGGED CROSS tune in my song "The Power of Love," including this stanza and refrain:

*Wisdom's pathways of peace, so despised by the world,*
*will save us from violence and death;*
*even though often mocked and rejected and scorned,*
*She keeps sending life-giving breath.*

*Still the power of Love casts out fear,*
*overcoming injustice and hate.*
*Now arise, for redemption draws near;*
*all creation can no longer wait.*

# The Gospel of the Female Divine

For many years I have been writing, preaching, and speaking on the power of the Female Divine to transform church and society. Female names and images of the Divine affirm the foundational biblical truth that female and male are created as equals in the divine image (Genesis 1:27). Including female names and images of Deity empowers us to live the good news of liberation, justice, equity, and peace.

The Female Divine brings the good news of the sacred value of all people. The intense feelings evoked by female divine names and images reveal their power. I have seen tears stream down the faces of women as they sing songs with female divine names and then say that this is the first time they have truly felt they are created in the divine image. The Female Divine also comes with good news for men and people of all genders striving to heal from sexism, racism, heterosexism, militarism, and classism.

Exploring connections between the Female Divine and social justice, I wrote *Changing Church: Stories of Liberating Ministers*.[9] For this book I interviewed twelve ministers of various races, genders, and denominations who include the Female Divine in songs and all aspects of liturgy. I discovered that this inclusive worship transforms the church and the wider culture, contributing to justice not only for women but for racial minorities, LGBTQIA+ persons, economically disadvantaged persons, and the earth. Seeking to learn more, I interviewed thirty-eight additional people, diverse in race and gender, for my book *She Lives! Sophia Wisdom Works in the World*.[10] The stories in this book also reveal that including the Female Divine in liturgy expands spiritual experience and supports gender equality, racial equality, marriage equality, economic justice, environmental justice, nonviolence, multifaith collaboration, and nonhierarchical structures.

Female names and images of the Divine help to dismantle patriarchal theology and structures that result in multiple, intersecting forms of oppression throughout the world. Female divine names and images contribute to our gospel mission of freeing all those oppressed (Luke 4:18). Reclaiming the Female Divine in our worship empowers our work together for equality, social justice, peace, and sustainability. Including multicultural female divine images in our sacred rituals affirms the sacred value of females of all races who continue to suffer from violence and abuse. President Jimmy Carter in *A Call to Action* declares that abuse of women and girls is the world's most serious and unaddressed violation of human rights, and he indicts patriarchal religion as this foundation for this abuse.[11] In *Half the Sky: Turning Oppression into Opportunity for Women Worldwide*, Sheryl WuDunn and Nicholas Kristof lament the "gendercide" resulting from violence inflicted routinely on women and girls in much of the world, which they call one of the "paramount human rights problems of this century."[12]

Genderless names and images of the Divine are not enough to deconstruct patriarchy and bring healing. Genderless language continues to allow socialized patterns of male dominance to shape values and actions. If all genders were valued and treated as equals, and if people perceived Deity to be female as well as male, nonbinary, and more, then genderless language could work. But all genders are not treated as equals, and this gender inequality has its foundation in prevalent exclusively male images of Deity. Just as the Black Lives Matter movement has taught us that, though all lives matter, we need to name that black lives matter because they have not mattered enough in our culture, so we need to name females in the divine image, though all genders are in the divine image, because the Female Divine has not been named and valued. Justice and equity come from naming that which has been unnamed, demeaned, devalued, and oppressed.

In *Inclusive Songs from the Heart of Gospel*, we name the Female Divine. We mine Scripture to reclaim Her many names, including "Wisdom" (*Hokmah* in the Hebrew Bible, Proverbs 1, 3, 4, 8, and *Sophia* in the Greek New Testament, 1 Corinthians 1:24, 30); "Mother" (Isaiah 49:15, 66:13); "Mother Eagle" (Deuteronomy 32:11–12); "Midwife" (Psalm 22:9–10); *Ruah* (Hebrew word for "Spirit," Genesis 1:2); *Shekhinah* (Hebrew word for "dwelling" presence of God, Exodus 29:45, 40:34–38); *Shaddai* (Hebrew word for "the Breasted God," Genesis 49:25). The song "We Celebrate Her Many Names" begins with this stanza:

*We celebrate Her many names: Sophia, Hokmah, Wisdom,*
*Shekhinah, Ruah, El Shaddai; Her names bring truth and freedom.*
*Too long Her names have been ignored, excluded, stifled, unexplored,*
*though found in Holy Scripture.*

One of the prominent female personifications of Deity in this songbook is *Ruah*. We find Her in the first chapter of the Bible, giving birth to the universe: "The Spirit (*Ruah*) moved over the face of the waters" (Genesis 1:2) to bring forth light and life. This female Creative Spirit at the beginning of biblical revelation has been buried in patriarchal culture and religious tradition. Resurrecting *Ruah* in our sacred songs will bring good news by revaluing what has been labeled and disparaged as "feminine" and empowering us all to embrace the wholeness of our creative gifts. One of the songs in this collection prays for the healing, re-creating power of *Ruah*, beginning with this stanza:

*Move throughout our world today,*
*Ruah, Breath of life, we pray;*
*Healing Wind, Transforming Fire,*
*re-create, restore, inspire.*
*Fill us with Your energy,*
*strength to work for equity;*
*when our path is hard and long,*
*lift our hearts with hopeful songs.*

The songs in this collection subvert the foundation of patriarchy through including female names and images of the Divine. As we sing these names and images in our sacred worship services, we spread the good news of liberation, justice, peace, and equity.

## The Gospel for All Races and All Genders

In *Inclusive Songs from the Heart of Gospel*, we highlight the intersection of gender justice and racial justice. We celebrate all races and all genders in the divine image. For example, the song "Come and See a Revelation" connects the affirmation of women's voices to the affirmation of all races and all genders as reflections of Divinity, concluding with this stanza:

*Open hearts and minds to visions; welcome revelations new.*
*Every race and every gender shows us all a wider view;*
*all reflect the sacred image; all reveal Divinity.*
*Come, explore unfolding wonders, filled with possibility.*

This song collection also contributes to racial justice and equity by changing the traditional symbolism of darkness as evil or ominous and light as good to symbolism of both darkness and light as good. These songs, like those in my other collections, affirm the sacred value of people of color in the divine image by giving positive meanings to images of darkness. For example, the song "Creative Darkness Fills the Earth" symbolizes darkness as birthing and nurturing all life, freeing us to create Beloved Community. "Our Sister Spirit" images the Divine as "dark and strong," lifting up Her "prophetic voice" to sound a call to freedom and justice. In "Sacred Darkness, Deep Within Us," we sing of darkness as creative bounty and beauty, concluding with this stanza:

*Sacred Darkness, deep within us, nurtures and creates new life;*
*flowing from Her rich abundance, seeds of justice bloom and thrive.*
*She illumines earth with beauty, marvelous diversity;*
*guided by Her revelations, we find true community.*

*Inclusive Songs from the Heart of Gospel* brings good news of welcome and affirmation to all genders, including LGBTQIA+ people and people of all gender expressions and gender identities. The inclusion of female and male and more in our naming of Deity supports justice for all genders. Still prevalent male-dominated worship language and imagery contribute to heterosexism and transphobia as well as to sexism by exalting the traditional "masculine" and devaluing any traits that have been traditionally labeled "feminine." This exclusively male symbolism forms a foundation for the exclusion, demeaning, assault, and abuse of LGBTQIA+ persons. Transgender women, especially Black and Latinx transgender women, suffer more fatal violence than any other LGBTQIA+ persons.[13] According to the Human Rights Campaign, Black transgender women are especially vulnerable because of "a toxic mix of transphobia, racism and misogyny."[14] Including female divine names and multicultural imagery will help to end this violence by reclaiming the sacred value of the "feminine" and the divine image in all genders and races.

Nonbinary persons are included in our affirmation of all genders in this song collection. The word "they" is now widely accepted as a singular, as well as plural, gender nonbinary pronoun. The song "Every Moment the Divine Gives

Life" refers to the Divine as "They." Using "They" as singular and plural, this song celebrates the sacred image in nonbinary persons as well as the multiplicity of Divinity: "Let *us* make humankind in our image, according to *our* likeness" (Genesis 1:26a). This song, also appropriate for multifaith settings, begins with this stanza:

*Every moment the Divine gives life;*
*They create all living beings,*
*gently nurturing and freeing;*
*every moment the Divine gives life.*

In this song collection other names for the Divine that provide a theological foundation for gender and racial equality include "Godde" and "Christ-Sophia." Many people use "Godde" as a reference to Deity to make equal connection between the male name "God" and the female name "Goddess." The name "Christ-Sophia" also images equality, inspiring social justice through shared power. "Christ-Sophia" comes from the biblical and historical link between Christ and Wisdom (*Sophia* in the Greek language of the Christian Scriptures). Balancing the male name "Christ" with the female name *Sophia* in referring to Divinity symbolizes the equal connection of genders in the divine image. Also, the image of "Christ-Sophia," drawing from Egyptian and Greek sacred symbols and from Judaism and Christianity, bridges races and religious traditions, thus providing a model for a society based on partnership instead of domination.[15] One song begins with a prayer for Christ-Sophia's power and includes this stanza affirming our work together for gender and racial equity:

*As partners we create a place*
*where everyone is free,*
*where every gender, every race*
*will find true equity.*

# The Gospel for All Creation

Inclusive songs bring good news for all creation. Songs that include female divine names and positive images of darkness affirm the sacred value of all genders, all races, and all creation. Environmental justice intersects with gender and racial justice.

The whole creation suffers from patriarchal and white supremacist theology that has at its foundation an image of a white male God. References to the earth are traditionally female, but the female is not often given sacred value. The earth's fertile soil is dark, but darkness is not often given sacred value. Like females, especially females of color, the earth continues to suffer exploitation, assault, and abuse.

In *Inclusive Songs from the Heart of Gospel,* biblical female divine names and sacred images of darkness connect the revaluing of females of all races to the revaluing of the earth. In "She Calls Everyone," we sing of joining *Sophia* Wisdom to "make creation whole." The song "We Are Building on Her Love Eternal" affirms *Ruah* Spirit's guidance of "our work to nurture life." Another song celebrates the power of Sacred Darkness to stir "our creativity" and to set "all creation free." One song in this collection praises *El Shaddai* for bringing good news to all genders, all races, and all creation, concluding with this stanza:

*She is Friend of all creation, El Shaddai;*
*She is Friend of all creation, El Shaddai;*
*She affirms in Her embrace every gender, every race,*
*welcomes all with jubilation, El Shaddai.*

Our hope and prayer is that *Inclusive Songs from the Heart of Gospel* will bring good news of justice, peace, equity, love, and new life. We pray that these songs will inspire communities and individuals in our healing, transforming work in the world. This new song collection comes to you with the invitation to join in singing and creating inclusive songs to celebrate the divine image in all genders, all races, and all creation.

# NOTES

1. Kendra Weddle and Jann Aldredge-Clanton, *Building Bridges: Letha Dawson Scanzoni and Friends* (Eugene, OR: Cascade, 2018).

2. Jann Aldredge-Clanton with composer Larry E. Schultz, *Inclusive Hymns for Liberating Christians* (Austin, TX: Eakin, 2006); *Inclusive Hymns for Liberation, Peace, and Justice* (Austin, TX: Eakin, 2011); *Earth Transformed with Music: Inclusive Songs for Worship* (Fort Worth, TX: Eakin, 2015); *Inclusive Songs for Resistance & Social Action* (Fort Worth, TX: Eakin, 2018).

3. Jann Aldredge-Clanton and Larry E. Schultz, *Imagine God! A Children's Musical Exploring and Expressing Images of God* (Garland, TX: Choristers Guild, 2004).

4. Jann Aldredge-Clanton and Larry E. Schultz, *Sing and Dance and Play with Joy! Inclusive Songs for Young Children* (Raleigh, NC: Lulu, 2009).

5. Jann Aldredge-Clanton and Larry E. Schultz, "Loving Friend of Everyone" (Garland, TX: Choristers Guild, 2004); "We Thank You, God, for Animal Friends" (Garland, TX: Choristers Guild, 2007); "Are You Good and Are You Strong?" (Van Nuys, CA: Alfred, 2008); "Gathered Here to Share Our Music" (LarryESchultz.com, 2012).

6. Kelly Brown Douglas, *What's Faith Got to Do with It? Black Bodies/Christian Souls* (Maryknoll, NY: Orbis, 2005), 100.

7. Elizabeth A. Johnson, *She Who Is: The Mystery of God in Feminist Theological Discourse* (New York: Crossroad), 159.

8. Delores S. Williams, *Sisters in the Wilderness: The Challenge of Womanist God-Talk* (Maryknoll, NY: Orbis, 2013), 143.

9. Jann Aldredge-Clanton, *Changing Church: Stories of Liberating Ministers* (Eugene, OR: Cascade, 2011).

10. Jann Aldredge-Clanton, *She Lives: Sophia Wisdom Works in the World* (Woodstock, VT: Skylight Paths, 2014).

11. Jimmy Carter, *A Call to Action: Women, Religion, Violence, and Power* (New York: Simon & Schuster, 2014), 3-4.

12. Nicholas D. Kristof and Sheryl WuDunn, *Half the Sky: Turning Oppression into Opportunity for Women Worldwide* (New York: Knopf, 2009), xiii, xvii.

13. Human Rights Campaign, "Violence Against the Transgender and Gender Non-Conforming Community in 2020," https://www.hrc.org/resources/violence-against-the-trans-and-gender-non-conforming-community-in-2020.

14. Erin Donaghue, "'Horrific Spike' in Fatal Violence Against Transgender Community," *CBS News* (July 14, 2020), https://www.cbsnews.com/news/transgender-community-fatal-violence-spike/.

15. For detailed analysis of the significance of the connection between Christ and *Sophia* in Scripture and Christian tradition, see Jann Aldredge-Clanton, *In Search of the Christ-Sophia: An Inclusive Christology for Liberating Christians* (Mystic, CT: Twenty-Third, 1995; Austin, TX: Eakin, 2004).

# Christ-Sophia, Give Us Wisdom

*Proverbs 3:17; 1 Corinthians 1:24*

1. Christ-Sophia, give us wisdom; show us Your just and peaceful way; O guide us to understand each other; fill us with kindness now, we pray.
2. Christ-Sophia, give us courage; fill us with hope in times like these; O guide us through every lonesome valley; bring us Your healing from disease.
3. Christ-Sophia, give us power; help us to join Your work of grace; O guide us on paths of liberation, freeing each gender and each race.

Words: Jann Aldredge-Clanton
Music: American folk hymn
Words © 2020 Jann Aldredge-Clanton.

LONESOME VALLEY
8.8.10.8

# 3 Come and See a Revelation

*John 4:7-42, 20:11-18; Luke 24:1-12*

1. "Come and see a rev-e-la-tion; come, ex-plore a Mys-ter-y;" hear the wom-an of Sa-mar-ia, shar-ing her e-piph-a-ny: "Drink from wells of Liv-ing Wa-ter, spring-ing to e-ter-nal life, quench-ing thirst now and for-ev-er, bring-ing peace so all may thrive."

2. Why are wom-en of-ten doubt-ed, and their words too long ig-nored? Why are wom-en still ex-clud-ed, and their sto-ries un-ex-plored? Wom-en first saw rev-e-la-tions, wit-nessed first the Liv-ing Word. When will ev-ery-one be-lieve them? When will wom-en's truth be heard?

3. O-pen hearts and minds to vi-sions; wel-come rev-e-la-tions new. Ev-ery race and ev-ery gen-der shows us all a wid-er view; all re-flect the sa-cred im-age; all re-veal Di-vin-i-ty. Come, ex-plore un-fold-ing won-ders, filled with pos-si-bil-i-ty.

Words: Jann Aldredge-Clanton
Music: Joshua Leavitt
Words © 2019 Jann Aldredge-Clanton.

PLEADING SAVIOR
8.7.8.7 D

# Come and Seek Sophia Wisdom    4
*Proverbs 3:13-17; 1 Corinthians 1:24*

1. Come and seek Sophia Wisdom; seek Her paths of peace and freedom; come and seek Sophia Wisdom; She is healing everyone who comes.
2. All the world is filled with trouble, desolation, pain, and struggle; all the world is filled with trouble; how we need Her healing, deep and full.
3. We can hear the children crying, long oppressed, abused, and dying; we can hear the children crying, and the mothers' mournful, pleading sighs.
4. She will guide our justice-making, and will keep our hearts from breaking; She will guide our justice-making, and will give us strength to stay awake.

*Refrain:* How we need Sophia Wisdom; how we need Sophia Wisdom; how we need Sophia Wisdom; She will help us make a peaceful home.

Words: Jann Aldredge-Clanton  
Music: John S. Norris  
Words © 2020 Jann Aldredge-Clanton.

NORRIS  
8.8.8.9 with refrain

# 5 Come, El Shaddai,* with Tender Care

*Genesis 49:25; Isaiah 43:1-2*

1. Come, El Shaddai, with tender care to calm our deepest fears; the storms are raging everywhere around the world and here.
2. Come, El Shaddai, and call our names, each one of every race; Your voice can still the floods and flames, and bring us healing grace.
3. Come, El Shaddai, with peaceful rest to ease our weary strain; Your comfort soothes all those distressed, and brings relief from pain.
4. Come, El Shaddai, to feed our souls from Your abundant store; Your loving-kindness overflows with blessings evermore.

Words: Jann Aldredge-Clanton
Music: Hugh Wilson
Words © 2020 Jann Aldredge-Clanton.

MARTYRDOM (also AVON)
8.6.8.6 (CM)

*El Shaddai* is a Hebrew name translated "God of the Breasts," "the Breasted God," or "God Almighty."

# Come, Give Us Power for Our Day    6
*1 Corinthians 1:24; Proverbs 3:17-18*

1. Come, give us power for our day; come, Christ-Sophia, come; the raging storms obscure our way, and we are far from home.
2. We wander in the wilderness, weighed down by stress and strife; come, Christ-Sophia, give us rest, and keep our hope alive.
3. We long to co-create with You a peaceful dwelling place, a place where all find life anew, a home for every race.
4. As partners we create a place where everyone is free, where every gender, every race will find true equity.
5. With Christ-Sophia we will rise together shore to shore, to lift our voices to the skies, rejoicing evermore.

Words: Jann Aldredge-Clanton  
Music: William Croft  
Words © 2019 Jann Aldredge-Clanton.

ST. ANNE  
8.6.8.6 (CM)

# Come Together, Celebrate

*Philippians 1:3-5; Colossians 3:16*

10

1. Come to-geth-er, cel-e-brate, re-joice on this most glo-rious day;
raise your voic-es, clap your hands, let or-ches-tra and or-gan play.
Sing in grat-i-tude for those who lead in mak-ing mu-sic ring,
fill-ing halls and sanc-tu-ar-ies, lift-ing hearts to soar on wings.

2. Cel-e-brate cre-a-tive tal-ents, o-ver-flow-ing in-to light,
hymns and an-thems, words and mu-sic; they com-pose both day and night.
Lib-er-at-ing Spir-it guid-ing, fill-ing them with en-er-gy,
they cre-ate a-bun-dant beau-ty, o-pening new re-al-i-ty.

3. Al-ways teach-ing, al-ways learn-ing, they in-spire both young and old,
blend-ing tal-ents, skills, ex-pres-sion, rep-e-ti-tion, vi-sions bold;
gifts un-fold, in-crease, and blos-som, stir-ring ev-ery-one who hears;
they ex-cel as ed-u-ca-tors, bring-ing joy for man-y years.

4. Cel-e-brate pro-phet-ic call-ing, min-is-ters of jus-tice-love,
all in-clud-ing, all af-firm-ing, led by ho-ly Heav-enly Dove.
Still ex-pand-ing ev-er for-ward, they up-lift all gifts to thrive,
joined with cos-mic strings in sound-ing mu-sic flow-ing through all life.

Words: Jann Aldredge-Clanton
Music: Ludwig van Beethoven
Words © 2021 Jann Aldredge-Clanton.

HYMN TO JOY
8.7.8.7 D

# 10a Come Together, Celebrate

*Philippians 1:3-5; Colossians 3:16*

1. Come together, celebrate, rejoice on this most glorious day;
raise your voices, clap your hands, let orchestra and organ play.
Sing in gratitude for those who lead in making music ring,

2. Celebrate creative talents, overflowing into light,
hymns and anthems, words and music; they compose both day and night.
Liberating Spirit guiding, filling them with energy,

3. Always teaching, always learning, they inspire both young and old,
blending talents, skills, expression, repetition, visions bold;
gifts unfold, increase, and blossom, stirring everyone who hears;

4. Celebrate prophetic calling, ministers of justice-love,
all-including, all-affirming, led by holy Heavenly Dove.
Still expanding ever forward, they uplift all gifts to thrive,

Words: Jann Aldredge-Clanton
Music: Larry E. Schultz
Words © 2021 Jann Aldredge-Clanton; Music © 2001 Larry E. Schultz.

SPIRIT DANCE
8.7.8.7 D

*Small notes are for keyboard.

# El Shaddai*

12

*Genesis 49:25; Isaiah 49:15, 66:13*

1. Praise the Source of life and heal-ing, El Shad-dai; (El Shad-dai;) praise the Source of life and heal-ing, El Shad-dai; (El Shad-dai;) She will nur-ture us each day, giv-ing lov-ing care al-ways, un-der-stand-ing all our feel-ings, El Shad-dai.
2. She is Moth-er of all liv-ing, El Shad-dai; (El Shad-dai;) She is Moth-er of all liv-ing, El Shad-dai; (El Shad-dai;) She sur-rounds us with Her love, deep with-in us and a-bove, al-ways guid-ing, al-ways giv-ing, El Shad-dai.
3. She is Giv-er of all bless-ings, El Shad-dai; (El Shad-dai;) She is Giv-er of all bless-ings, El Shad-dai; (El Shad-dai;) She will show-er us with gifts that em-pow-er and up-lift, keep-ing ev-ery-one pro-gress-ing, El Shad-dai.
4. She is Friend of all cre-a-tion, El Shad-dai; (El Shad-dai;) She is Friend of all cre-a-tion, El Shad-dai; (El Shad-dai;) She af-firms in Her em-brace ev-ery gen-der, ev-ery race, wel-comes all with ju-bi-la-tion, El Shad-dai.

Words: Jann Aldredge-Clanton
Music: Charles Albert Tindley
Words © 2019 Jann Aldredge-Clanton.

*El Shaddai* is a Hebrew name translated "God of the Breasts," "the Breasted God," or "God Almighty."

STAND BY ME
8.3.8.3.7.7.8.3

# 13 Ever Embracing ∞ Ever Becoming

1. Ever embracing, caring and serving, eagerly greeting each person as friend, we give to all a wide-open welcome, sharing a lifetime of love without end.
2. Ever becoming, learning and growing, mindfully shaping our life yet to be, we search for Wisdom, always evolving, joyfully finding new ways to be free.
3. "Ever embracing, Ever becoming," this is the heart-song inspiring our days. We sing it out through all generations, gratefully joining our voices in praise!

Words: Larry E. Schultz  
Music: Larry E. Schultz  
Words and Music © 2021 Larry E. Schultz.

FAYETTEVILLE STREET  
10.10.10.10

# Every Moment the Divine Gives Life    14

*Genesis 1:20-27*

Words: Jann Aldredge-Clanton
Music: William G. Tomer
Words © 2019 Jann Aldredge-Clanton.

GOD BE WITH YOU
9.8.8.9 with refrain

*"They" is now widely accepted as a singular,
as well as plural, gender nonbinary pronoun.

# 15 Friend of All
*John 15:15*

1. Come to the Friend who will bring us heal-ing, Friend of all, Friend of all;
2. Come to the Friend who will al-ways hear us, Friend of all, Friend of all;
3. Come to the Friend who in-spires our grow-ing, Friend of all, Friend of all;
4. She wel-comes all in Her kind em-brac-es, Friend of all, Friend of all;

She un-der-stands ev-ery pain-ful feel-ing, Friend of all, Friend of all.
Her lov-ing pres-ence is al-ways near us, Friend of all, Friend of all.
Her ten-der pow-er is al-ways flow-ing, Friend of all, Friend of all.
Her gen-tle call stirs our gifts and grac-es, Friend of all, Friend of all.

She in-cludes ev-ery race and gen-der, tak-ing down ev-ery sti-fling wall; come to the Friend who will bring us heal-ing, Friend of all, Friend of all.

Words: Jann Aldredge-Clanton
Music: George C. Hugg
Words © 2019 Jann Aldredge-Clanton.

HARPER MEMORIAL
10.6.10.6 with refrain

# Gather Everywhere in Circles 16
*Galatians 5:22*

1. Come and gather now in circles, where we all have equal worth; come, tell stories now in circles, sharing sadness, hope, and mirth.
2. Feel the Spirit freely flowing in our circles deep and wide; joined with Her we keep on growing, sharing visions side by side.
3. Through our circles we are giving hope to change the world today; with the Spirit in us living, we create Her peaceful ways.

*Refrain:* Gather everywhere in circles, in healing and empowering circles; join the Spirit moving in circles, where every voice will be heard.

Words: Jann Aldredge-Clanton
Music: Robert Lowry
Words © 2018 Jann Aldredge-Clanton.

HANSON PLACE
8.7.8.7 with refrain

# Guiding on Healing Paths
*Exodus 29:45, 40:34-38*

18

1. Shekhinah* dwells in everyone, guiding on healing paths;
   She moves from night to rising sun, guiding on healing paths.
2. Shekhinah keeps us brave and strong, guiding on healing paths;
   She helps in overcoming wrong, guiding on healing paths.
3. Shekhinah gives us energy, guiding on healing paths;
   Her power builds community, guiding on healing paths.

*Refrain:*
Shekhinah, sacred Presence, shows us Her healing paths;
Her glory shines around us, guiding on healing paths.

Words: Jann Aldredge-Clanton
Music: Cleland Boyd McAfee
Words © 2020 Jann Aldredge-Clanton.

McAFEE
8.6.8.6 (CM) with refrain

*Shekhinah* is a feminine Hebrew word translated "dwelling" or "settling," and is used to denote the dwelling presence of the Divine and/or the glory of the Divine.

# 19  Hear Her Urgent Cry
*Proverbs 1:20-23, 3:17; Amos 5:24*

1. How long must Wisdom cry for peace? Hear Her urgent cry:
"When will injustice ever cease?" Hear Her urgent cry.
2. Now Wisdom calls for true reforms; hear Her urgent cry:
"Come, join to change oppressive norms." Hear Her urgent cry.
3. Still Wisdom longs to set us free; hear Her urgent cry:
"Come, join Beloved Community." Hear Her urgent cry.

Come to Her peaceful way, bringing life anew;
choose Her justice-love today, Her transforming view.

Words: Jann Aldredge-Clanton
Music: William J. Kirkpatrick
Words © 2020 Jann Aldredge-Clanton.

COMING HOME
8.5.8.5 with refrain

# Hokmah* Wisdom Shows the Way    20

*Exodus 1:15-22; Micah 6:4*

1. Hok-mah Wisdom shows the way through the wilderness today; She will keep our spirits strong, giving us a hopeful song.
2. Hok-mah Wisdom long ago guided Hebrew midwives bold; Puah, Shiphrah saved the boys, thwarted evil Pharaoh's ploy.
3. Miriam and Moses led when the Hebrew people fled; Hokmah Wisdom's powerful hand guided to the Promised Land.
4. Hok-mah Wisdom liberates, calling us to co-create; She will give us all we need when we plant Her justice seeds.

Words: Jann Aldredge-Clanton  
Music: *Enchiridia*, Erfurt, 1524; harm. Seth Calvisius  
Words © 2020 Jann Aldredge-Clanton.

NUN KOMM DER HEIDEN HEILAND  
7.7.7.7

*Hokmah is the word for "Wisdom" in the Hebrew Scriptures.

# 21 Holy Wisdom Calls

*Proverbs 1:20-23, 3:13-18; Amos 5:22-24*

1. When will oppression and violence cease? When will we see Wisdom's truth increase? She is the path to a world of peace; Holy Wisdom calls.
2. How long will hatred and fear hold sway? When will we all follow Wisdom's way? She guides us forward to peaceful days; Holy Wisdom calls.
3. Come, join with Wisdom to end the strife; follow Her pathways for all to thrive; She leads us on to abundant life; Holy Wisdom calls.

*Refrain:* Holy Wisdom calls, Holy Wisdom calls; She is the path to a world of peace; Holy Wisdom calls.

Words: Jann Aldredge-Clanton
Music: John H. Stockton
Words © 2019 Jann Aldredge-Clanton.

GLORY TO HIS NAME
9.9.9.5 with refrain

# Holy Wisdom Fills Our Hearts with Song  22
*Proverbs 3:13-18*

1. Holy Wisdom fills our hearts with song, overcoming all our fear; She will give us hope through days so long, helping us to persevere. Sing of Holy Wisdom, calling out today, longing to bring healing, showing us Her loving way.
2. All around the sound of violence rings; discord fills the world with pain; Holy Wisdom heals the broken strings, bringing harmony again. Sing of Holy Wisdom, calling out today, longing to bring healing, showing us Her loving way.
3. Songs and stories heal and liberate, setting all our voices free; rising up together we create Holy Wisdom's symphony. Sing of Holy Wisdom, calling out today, longing to bring healing, showing us Her loving way.

Words: Jann Aldredge-Clanton
Music: Luther B. Bridgers
Words © 2018 Jann Aldredge-Clanton.

SWEETEST NAME
9.7.9.7 with refrain

# 23 In Her Power We Are Rising

*Deuteronomy 32:11-12*

1. In Her power we are rising; Mother Eagle lifts us high, giving energy surprising, as we're reaching up to fly. In Her power we are rising; Mother Eagle lifts us high, giving marvelous surprises, as we soar throughout the sky.

2. When we feel distressed and weary, Mother Eagle gives us care; calming all our doubt and fearing, She restores our faith to dare.

3. In Her grace we are abounding; Mother Eagle guides our flight, bringing miracles astounding, as we're stretching to new heights.

Words: Jann Aldredge-Clanton
Music: P. P. Bilhorn
Words © 2020 Jann Aldredge-Clanton.

WONDROUS STORY
8.7.8.7 with refrain

# 25 Join All Together As One

Acts 1:8; Romans 15:13

1. As we join hands on a mis-sion of peace, pray-ing that our cour-age
will in-crease, the Spir-it gives us en-er-gy on Her mis-sion of peace.
2. As we join hands on a mis-sion of grace, lift-ing up each gen-der
and each race, the Spir-it gives us lib-er-ty on Her mis-sion of grace.
3. As we join hands on a mis-sion of love, draw-ing on Her pow-er
from a-bove, the Spir-it gives us syn-er-gy on Her mis-sion of love.

Come, come, all peo-ple, come; let's join hands, ev-ery-one;
come, come, all peo-ple, come; join all to-geth-er as one.

Words: Jann Aldredge-Clanton
Music: American folk song; arr. Larry E. Schultz
Words © 2019 Jann Aldredge-Clanton; Music arr. © 2021 Larry E. Schultz.

DOWN TO THE RIVER
10.9.8.6 with refrain

# Join to Create

26

1. Join to create places free and fair, where every-one can thrive; come, hand in hand; join with Wisdom there, keeping our hope alive.
2. Join to create places true and kind; justice awaits us there; Wisdom will guide every-one to find visions and dreams to share.
3. Join to create places filled with love, following Wisdom's voice; She sings to us like a gentle dove, making our hearts rejoice.

Refrain:
Join to create peace every-where; join Wisdom's plan, spreading Her loving care.
Join to create, join to create peace every-where, peace every-where; join Wisdom's plan, join Wisdom's plan, loving care.

Words: McKenzie Brown and Jann Aldredge-Clanton
Music: Charles E. Moody
Words © 2019 McKenzie Brown and Jann Aldredge-Clanton.

KNEEL AT THE CROSS
9.6.9.6 with refrain

# 27. Keeping Hope Alive

*Isaiah 66:13; Romans 8:24-25*

1. We're tired of staying strong and tough, while trying hard to do enough; when hurtful words bring pain and strife, we struggle keeping hope alive.
2. Sometimes we feel that no one cares about the work we try to share. Can we still find the faith to strive and strength for keeping hope alive?
3. We find a new community with common dreams of equity; now we can feel our hearts revive, together keeping hope alive.

O Mother Godde,* help us to know Your tender power in us flows; give us the energy to thrive, as we are keeping hope alive.

Words: Jann Aldredge-Clanton
Music: Charles H. Gabriel
Words © 2019 Jann Aldredge-Clanton.

HIGHER GROUND
8.8.8.8 (LM) with refrain

*"Godde" is a term some Christian feminists use in referring to Deity, combining the male name "God" and the female name "Goddess."

# Liberating Christ-Sophia

*Luke 4:18; 1 Corinthians 1:24*

28

1. Come to take away our fear, liberating Christ-Sophia;
come to bring us hope and cheer, liberating Christ-Sophia.
2. In these times we need Your power, liberating Christ-Sophia;
guide us through this urgent hour, liberating Christ-Sophia.
3. Give us courage every day, liberating Christ-Sophia;
fill us all with strength, we pray, liberating Christ-Sophia.
4. Spread Your beauty through the earth, liberating Christ-Sophia;
we will join to bring rebirth, liberating Christ-Sophia.

Come, bring us peace today; show us Your healing way,
forever with us stay, liberating Christ-Sophia.

Words: Jann Aldredge-Clanton
Music: Robert Lowry
Words © 2020 Jann Aldredge-Clanton.

PLAINFIELD
7.8.7.8 with refrain

# 29 Liberating Spirit Calls

Matthew 3:16; 2 Timothy 1:7

1. Lib-er-at-ing Spir-it sounds the call, "Join my work of eq-ui-ty; take down each di-vid-ing, sti-fling wall, set-ting all cre-a-tion free."
2. Though our path-way winds through rock-y land, Lib-er-a-ting Spir-it leads, guid-ing us to jour-ney hand in hand, giv-ing ev-ery-thing we need.
3. Lib-er-at-ing Spir-it gives us power, mak-ing dreams re-al-i-ty, stir-ring all our gifts to ful-ly flower, bring-ing peace and har-mo-ny.

Lib-er-a-ting Spir-it guides us all a-long, fills our hearts with cour-age, keeps us sing-ing free-dom songs.

Words: Jann Aldredge-Clanton
Music: Luther B. Bridgers
Words © 2020 Jann Aldredge-Clanton.

SWEETEST NAME
9.7.9.7 with refrain

# Longing for Healing Peace 30

*Proverbs 1:20-23, 3:17*

1. Through-out these per-il-ous days, when threat of dan-ger holds sway, and fear is block-ing our way, we are long-ing for heal-ing peace.
2. In times like these we de-cry that truth is trad-ed for lies, and jus-tice-love is de-nied; we are long-ing for heal-ing peace.
3. Still Wis-dom sounds Her clear call to take down lim-it-ing walls, and o-pen wel-com-ing halls; we are long-ing for heal-ing peace.

Long-ing for heal-ing peace, we are long-ing for heal-ing peace; we will seek Wis-dom's ways, fol-low Her to new days; we are long-ing for heal-ing peace.

Words: Jann Aldredge-Clanton
Music: Charles E. Moody
Words © 2020 Jann Aldredge-Clanton.

OUT ON THE PERILOUS DEEP
7.7.7.8 with refrain

# 31 Loving Shepherd Comes to Guide Us
*Psalm 23*

1. Loving Shepherd comes to guide us with strong and tender hand; She will lead us safely through these troubled times; our Faithful Friend is with us through every rocky land, giving strength for every mountain we must
2. Loving Shepherd feels our sorrows, and understands our pain; She will hold us gently calming every fear, sharing all our heavy burdens to lighten stress and strain; in the midst of struggles She is always
3. Loving Shepherd goes before us, preparing peaceful ways; by the tranquil waters She restores our souls; through verdant meadows leading to healing day by day, She is guiding us to make creation

Words: Jann Aldredge-Clanton  
Music: William S. Hays  
Words © 2020 Jann Aldredge-Clanton.

SALVATIONIST  
Irregular with refrain

# Move Throughout Our World Today     33
*Genesis 1; Acts 2:1-17*

1. Move throughout our world today, Ruah,* Breath of Life, we pray;
Healing Wind, Transforming Fire, re-create, restore, inspire.
Fill us with Your energy, strength to work for equity,
when our path is hard and long, lift our hearts with hopeful song.

2. Ruah, Spirit, Breath of Life, change our world so all survive;
violent forces raging still traumatize, assault, and kill.
Help us stop the violence now; give us guidance, show us how;
stir within our minds and hearts healing power to impart.

3. Ruah, Spirit, Breath of Life, breathe in all to end the strife;
send renewing harmony, justice-love and liberty.
Challenge us to stretch and grow, claim divine creative flow;
nurture our diversity, forming true community.

Words: Jann Aldredge-Clanton
Music: Ferdinand Hérold
Words © 2020 Jann Aldredge-Clanton.

MESSIAH
7.7.7.7 D

*Ruah* is the word for "Spirit" in the Hebrew Scriptures.

# 34 New Life Awaits Us All
*John 8:32; Acts 2:17*

1. New life awaits us all along the gospel way; we're growing and becoming stronger every day. We join with people rising up on every shore, and we keep on embracing new life evermore.

2. We will not let abusive systems keep us down; they cannot stop us now, for we are freedom bound. The Spirit deep within gives energy to soar, and we keep on embracing new life evermore.

3. The Spirit gives us visions of equality; Her power sets us free to be all we can be. We join together, moving onward to explore, and we keep on embracing new life evermore.

Words: Jann Aldredge-Clanton  
Music: Albert E. Brumley  
Words © 2019 Jann Aldredge-Clanton.

THIS WORLD IS NOT MY HOME  
12.12.12.12 with refrain

# 36. O Mother Godde*

1. O Mother Godde, at end of day I ponder, and think of all the things Your hands have made. The deep night sky above the city's thunder relieves the stress and struggles of my day.

2. When through my town and neighborhood I wander, I feel a pulse, the rhythm of our lives. I think of many paths where we may linger; we all are seeking places we can thrive.

3. I think of how each day our varied lives flow, traveling on subways, highways, and the streets. Each has such depth; we all have pain we don't show; each one is struggling, trying to be free.

4. One day we'll rise above our daily worries, and we'll become all we are meant to be. With Mother Godde we'll journey, never hurried; our troubled minds at last will be at ease.

Words: McKenzie Brown and Jann Aldredge-Clanton  
Music: Swedish folk melody  
Words © 2018 McKenzie Brown and Jann-Aldredge Clanton.

O STORE GUD  
11.10.11.10 with refrain

*"Godde" is a term some Christian feminists use in referring to Deity, combining the male name "God" and the female name "Goddess."

# 37. O Mother Godde,* I Come

1. Just as I am, though lost at sea, Her love will light a way for me, and put my weary mind at ease;
2. Just as I am, with doubts and fears that mold-ed me through-out the years, She shares each sorrow, every tear;
3. Just as I am, She helps me see how worthy She cre-at-ed me; I close my eyes, She says "just be";
4. Just as I am, She will embrace, will welcome, love, and offer grace, and at the end of every day,

O Mother Godde, I come, I come.
O Mother Godde, I come, I come.
O Mother Godde, I come, I come.
O Mother Godde, I'll come, I'll come.

Words: McKenzie Brown
Music: William B. Bradbury
Words © 2018 McKenzie Brown.

WOODWORTH
8.8.8.8 (LM)

*"Godde" is a term some Christian feminists use in referring to Deity, combining the male name "God" and the female name "Goddess."

# 39. Our Mother Inspires All Our Work

*Deuteronomy 32:11-12; Isaiah 49:15*

1. Our Mother inspires all our work in the world, restoring, creating each day; She fills us with courage to labor with Her, illumining Her peaceful way.

2. The world is now wounded from violence and greed, and all of our efforts seem lost; our Mother supplies us with strength to endure, persisting whatever the cost.

3. Our Mother still calls us to join in Her work for all of creation to thrive; She comes to revive us and nurture our souls with visions to keep hope alive.

Words: Jann Aldredge-Clanton
Music: William J. Kirkpatrick
Words © 2019 Jann Aldredge-Clanton.

KIRKPATRICK
11.8.11.8 with refrain

# Our Sister Spirit

*Proverbs 1:20-23; Isaiah 45:3; Matthew 25:35-40*

41

1. Our Sister Spirit, dark and strong, lifts up prophetic voice; we find Her in each freedom song, in every justice choice.
2. Our Sister Spirit, brave and small, lifts up Her urgent cries; we find Her at the border wall, in children's lonely eyes.
3. Our Sister Spirit, tired and poor, lifts up Her cry of stress; we find Her on the factory floor, in workers long distressed.
4. Our Sister Spirit, old and bold, lifts up Her wisdom words; we find Her in the truth foretold, in peaceful message heard.

Words: Jann Aldredge-Clanton
Music: American folk melody; arr. Larry E. Schultz
Words © 2019 Jann Aldredge-Clanton; Music arr. © 2022 Larry E. Schultz.

LAND OF REST
8.6.8.6 (CM)

# 42

## Pillar of Salt
*Genesis 19:1-26*

With the strength of Lot's wife find the strength to look back: without fear for your life, without fear of attack. If we live in compassion our footsteps will

Words: Larry E. Schultz
Music: Larry E. Schultz
Words and Music © 2019 Larry E. Schultz.

CRISP
12.12.12.10.11

*The small notes in this measure and where found in the 1st & 2nd Endings are for keyboard and the large notes for voices.

# 43 Power in Us All

*Proverbs 3:13-18; Amos 5:24*

1. Wisdom within us is boundless and free; there's power in us all, power in us all; She moves us forward to all we can be; there's life-giving power in us all.
2. Though we are weary from laboring long, there's power in us all, power in us all; Wisdom will help us to overcome wrong; there's life-giving power in us all.
3. Would you be free from the voices of doubt? There's power in us all, power in us all; Wisdom will give us the strength to speak out; there's life-giving power in us all.
4. When we are working for justice and peace, there's power in us all, power in us all; Wisdom within us will daily increase; there's life-giving power in us all.

Words: Jann Aldredge-Clanton
Music: Lewis E. Jones
Words © 2018 Jann Aldredge-Clanton.

POWER IN THE BLOOD
10.9.10.8 with refrain

# Sacred Darkness, Deep Within Us 46
*Isaiah 45:3*

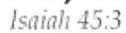

1. Sa-cred Dark-ness, deep with-in us, stirs our cre-a-tiv-i-ty,
2. Sa-cred Dark-ness guides our jour-ney, lead-ing to e-qual-i-ty,
3. Sa-cred Dark-ness, deep with-in us, nur-tures and cre-ates new life;

o-pening up Her hid-den treas-ures, far be-yond all we can see.
show-ing how to end op-pres-sion, set-ting all cre-a-tion free.
flow-ing from Her rich a-bun-dance, seeds of jus-tice bloom and thrive.

As we move in-to our cen-ter, glo-rious mir-a-cles un-fold,
She will give us strength for ac-tion, cour-age as we work for change,
She il-lu-mines earth with beau-ty, mar-vel-ous di-ver-si-ty;

giv-ing us new in-spi-ra-tion, pow-er to be brave and bold.
break-ing walls and build-ing bridg-es, peace-ful pat-terns to ar-range.
guid-ed by Her rev-e-la-tions, we find true com-mu-ni-ty.

Words: Jann Aldredge-Clanton
Music: Ananias Davisson's *Supplement to the Kentucky Harmony*, 1820, alt.; arr. Larry E. Schultz
Words © 2019 Jann Aldredge-Clanton; Music arr. © 2021 Larry E. Schultz

JUBILEE, alt.
8.7.8.7 D

# 47  She Calls Everyone
*Proverbs 1:20-21, 3:17-18*

1. So-phi-a Wis-dom gen-tly calls to ev-ery-one, ex-clud-ing none; She takes down ob-sta-cles and walls, and calls ev-ery-one. She calls+ ev-ery-one; She calls ev-ery-one; So-phi-a calls; She calls ev-ery-one.
2. So-phi-a Wis-dom la-bors long so peace and jus-tice will be done; we join Her work a-gainst the wrong, and free ev-ery-one. calls+ ev-ery-one, calls ev-ery-one, calls ev-ery-one, So-phi-a calls,+ So-phi-a calls;
3. So-phi-a Wis-dom in our souls will guide our work till kin-dom* comes; with Her we make cre-a-tion whole, and heal ev-ery-one. calls ev-ery-one; calls ev-ery-one, ev-ery-one.

+2nd Refrain: She *frees* everyone.
3rd Refrain: She *heals* everyone.

Words: Jann Aldredge-Clanton
Music: J. Calvin Bushey
Words © 2020 Jann Aldredge-Clanton.

CALVIN
8.8.8.5 with refrain

*The word "kin-dom" is an inclusive alternative to "kingdom"; "kin-dom" emphasizes the nonsexist, nonclassist nature of the divine realm and underscores our common kinship with the Divine and one another.

# She Will Heal Us 48
*Matthew 3:16; Romans 8:26-27*

1. The Spirit moves within our world, around us and above; She comes with healing wings unfurled, the holy Heavenly Dove.
2. The Spirit longs to heal our world from violence and unrest; when hateful, harmful words are hurled, She sides with those oppressed.
3. The Spirit stirs us now to go to spread Her loving care, and Her restoring grace will flow with life beyond compare.

Follow now the loving Spirit; She will show us how;
She will heal us; She will heal us; She will heal us now.

Words: Jann Aldredge-Clanton
Music: John H. Stockton
Words © 2020 Jann Aldredge-Clanton.

STOCKTON
8.6.8.6 (CM) with refrain

# 49 Shekhinah* Is Shining on Earth
*Exodus 40:34-38*

1. We are sowing equality, justice, and peace, helping all to reclaim sacred worth. We envision that kindness and love will increase, as Shekhinah is shining on earth.
2. Through the world exploitation and violence persist; all creation is suffering today. We are coming together to rise and resist, as Shekhinah is showing the way.
3. What a joy we discover when change has begun, as we labor with hope for new birth. Day by day we will keep sowing seeds one by one, as Shekhinah is shining on earth.

Words: Jann Aldredge-Clanton
Music: John R. Sweney
Words © 2019 Jann Aldredge-Clanton.

STARS IN MY CROWN
12.9.12.9 with refrain

*Shekhinah* is a feminine Hebrew word translated "dwelling" or "settling," and is used to denote the dwelling presence of the Divine and/or the glory of the Divine.

# 50   Sister Spirit Shows the Healing Way
*1 Corinthians 12:4-11*

1. When we can-not find our way through the long and gloom-y days, we are fear-ful and dis-cour-aged, heav-y-heart-ed, and dis-mayed. Sis-ter Spir-it comes to guide; She is al-ways by our side, clear-ly show-ing us a path that o-pens wide.

2. When our la-bor seems in vain and we feel the stress and strain, we keep work-ing to dis-man-tle sys-tems caus-ing so much pain, and no mat-ter how we try, man-y ef-forts go a-wry, but we know that Sis-ter Spir-it hears our cry.

3. Ev-ery day a-round the world hate-ful mes-sag-es are hurled; we will o-ver-come with love and peace-ful ban-ners now un-furled. Sis-ter Spir-it takes down walls, giv-ing cour-age when we call; we will join Her work of lib-er-at-ing all.

Words: Jann Aldredge-Clanton
Music: Charles A. Tindley; arr. B.B. McKinney
Words © 2019 Jann Aldredge-Clanton.

BY AND BY
7.7.8.7.7.7.11 with refrain

## 51. Sister-Brother Spirit Sets Us Free

*2 Corinthians 3:17; Galatians 5:22*

1. Every day we find so many bound, stifled by oppression all around. When will people everywhere be found in liberty?
2. Sister-Brother Spirit, wise and strong, gives us energy for righting wrong; rising up together, we all long for liberty.
3. Sister-Brother Spirit, kind and fair, comes to change the world with loving care, so that everyone at last can share in liberty.

*Refrain:*
Sister-Brother Spirit sets us free, bringing justice, peace, and unity; now our voices sing in harmony of liberty.

Words: Jann Aldredge-Clanton
Music: Daniel B. Towner
Words © 2020 Jann Aldredge-Clanton.

CALVARY
9.9.9.4 with refrain

# So Many People Cry in Pain 52

*Proverbs 1:7, 20-23, 3:17*

1. So many people cry in pain, exploited and abused.
Has Wisdom's message been in vain, and all Her ways refused,
and all Her ways refused, and all Her ways refused?

2. When will we all at last be free from violence, hate, and fear?
With Wisdom we find liberty; Her saving power is near.
Her saving power is near; Her saving power is near.

3. She keeps on calling out for peace, though often mocked and scorned;
Her loving power will still increase, and all will be reborn,
and all will be reborn, and all will be reborn.

Words: Jann Aldredge-Clanton  
Music: Early American melody  
Words © 2019 Jann Aldredge-Clanton.

CLEANSING FOUNTAIN  
8.6.8.6.6.6.8.6

# 53. Sophia Wisdom Gives Us Power

*Proverbs 3:13-18, 4:8-9*

1. Sophia Wisdom gives us power to open every door, to open every door; with Her all people fully flower,
2. Sophia Wisdom brings new life and peace on every shore, and peace on every shore; with Her all people fully thrive,
3. Sophia Wisdom crowns our days with wonders to explore, with wonders to explore; we follow Her transforming ways,

Words: Jann Aldredge-Clanton
Music: James Ellor
Words © 2020 Jann Aldredge-Clanton.

DIADEM
8.6.6.8 with refrain

## 54 Spirit of Godde,* Spark of Creation

1. Spirit of Godde, spark of creation, glowing in all, burning and bright, fire on the mountain and flame on the altar,
2. Deeply within, seemingly silent, working unseen, life-giving source, particles vibrating, pulsing, expanding,
3. Whispering voice, inner discernment, for every choice, thoughtful and clear, channel of Wisdom, conveyor of feeling,
4. Always beside, constant companion, going before, guarding behind, eversurrounding, supporting, inspiring,
5. Powerful wind, suddenly surging, breaking down walls till there are none, sweeping us forward with dreams and new visions,

Words: Larry E. Schultz
Music: Larry E. Schultz
Words and Music © 2012 Larry E. Schultz.

RENEWAL
Irregular

*Combining the male designation, "God," and the female, "Goddess," "Godde" is a term for divinity that transcends gender.

# 55 Spirit of Life and Love

*Genesis 1; Romans 8:2*

1. Spir-it of Life and Love moves through-out the earth, nur-tur-ing and birth-ing;
2. Spir-it of Life and Love, re-cre-a-ting Source, stops de-struc-tive forc-es,
3. Spir-it of Life and Love dwells in ev-ery race, pour-ing out Her grac-es;

Spir-it of Life and Love deep with-in us flows, more than we can know.
call-ing us now to join Her to end op-pres-sion and all dis-tress.
Spir-it of Life and Love frees each one to soar, open-ing ev-ery door.

She gives us hope and heal-ing, stir-ring our deep-est feel-ings;

She fills us with Her pow-er for trans-for-ma-tion each day and hour.

Words: Jann Aldredge-Clanton
Music: Swedish folk tune; arr. Larry E. Schultz
Words © 2020 Jann Aldredge-Clanton; Music arr. © 2022 Larry E. Schultz.

VÅRVINDAR FRISKA
11.6.11.5 with refrain

## 58 The Power of Love

*Proverbs 1:7, 20-23, 3:17; 1 John 4:18*

1. In our world everywhere people suffer abuse, as evil too often holds sway. Wisdom lovingly calls, but so many refuse to follow Her transforming way.
2. Wisdom's pathways of peace, so despised by the world, will save us from violence and death; even though often mocked and rejected and scorned, She keeps sending life-giving breath.
3. Still our wounded world groans, overburdened with pain, weighed down with oppression and strife. Wisdom suffers with all, and She helps us regain our hope in abundant new life.

Words: Jann Aldredge-Clanton
Music: George Bennard
Words © 2019 Jann Aldredge-Clanton.

OLD RUGGED CROSS
12.8.12.8 with refrain

# There's Justice Work for Us to Do 60

1. O my neighbor, have you met our Mother, who will guide us to seek truth? Follow Her on peaceful pathways; there's justice work for us to do.
2. Have you ever witnessed Mother's power? She will help tired souls feel new. She rejuvenates, revives us; there's justice work for us to do.
3. Do you look around the world and wonder if good-will is over-due? We must care, and work repairing; there's justice work for us to do.
4. As you go out look to Her for guidance; trust that She will see you through. Every day She shows us Her way; there's justice work for us to do.

Refrain: Oh, there's justice work to do, my neighbor; there's justice work for us to do. Dreams of peace vitalize our labor; there's justice work for us to do.

Words: McKenzie Brown  
Music: F. A. Graves  
Words © 2019 McKenzie Brown.

O MY BROTHER, DO YOU KNOW THE SAVIOR  
10.7.8.8 with refrain

# 61 They Who Wait
*Isaiah 40:31*

1. They who wait, they who wait, shall renew their strength, shall renew their strength, on the wind spread their wings, till their spirits soar, till their spirits sing.

2. We who wait, we who wait, shall renew our strength, shall renew our strength, on the wind spread our wings, till our spirits soar, till our spirits sing. Wait. Wait. Wait.

Words: Isaiah 40:31; Larry E. Schultz
Music: Larry E. Schultz
Words and Music © 2021 Larry E. Schultz.

WAIT
6.10.6.10

# We Are Building on Her Love Eternal  62

1. We are build-ing on Her Love e-ter-nal, guid-ed by Her lib-er-at-ing hand.
2. We are build-ing on a strong foun-da-tion, through the tri-als, through the pain and strife.
3. We are build-ing on a strong foun-da-tion, an-chored in Her Love that makes us whole.
4. We are build-ing on a strong foun-da-tion, build-ing high-er up and tak-ing stock.

Do you see the change, not just ex-ter-nal, as we fol-low Ru-ah* Spir-it's plan?
We are build-ing for a new cre-a-tion; She will guide our work to nur-ture life.
We are build-ing jus-tice in each na-tion, so that peace through-out the world will flow.
We are ground-ed in Her rev-e-la-tion; Ru-ah Spir-it stands as our firm rock.

We are build-ing on Her Love; we are build-ing on Her Love; we are build-ing on Her Love, our jus-tice dreams in hand.

Words: McKenzie Brown and Jann Aldredge-Clanton  
Music: Barney Elliott Warren  
Words © 2020 McKenzie Brown and Jann Aldredge-Clanton.

ARE YOU BUILDING ON THE ROCK ETERNAL  
10.9.10.9 with refrain  
*Ruah* is the word for "Spirit"  
in the Hebrew Scriptures.

# 63 We Are Dreaming of a World
*Galatians 5:22*

1. We are dreaming of a world of equality; we are dreaming of a world filled with peace. Now the Spirit gives us visions of what can be; joined with Her our justice work will increase.

2. We are working for a world where all children thrive, where they grow up to be all they can be; we are joining all together to march for lives. "Stop the violence," we cry out urgently.

3. We are calling for a world that is safe and fair, where we all can have the freedom of choice. We are rising up together as we declare, "Time's Up! Give us equal rights, equal voice."

4. We are singing of a world filled with love for all, where we open doors and welcome each one. Now the Spirit gives us power to take down walls; we will labor so Her kin-dom* will come.

Words: Jann Aldredge-Clanton
Music: J. K. Alwood
Words © 2018 Jann Aldredge-Clanton.

THE UNCLOUDED DAY
12.10.12.10 with refrain

*The word "kin-dom" is an inclusive alternative to "kingdom"; "kin-dom" emphasizes the nonsexist, nonclassist nature of the divine realm and underscores our common kinship with the Divine and one another.

# 64. We Are Rising Up Together

1. I was standing, with convictions but alone from day to day.
And I wondered, were there others who could help me find my way?

2. Then one day I found my people, for the first time, unconstrained.
We rejoiced and started planning how to ease the world of pain.

3. As we parted, we felt sadness, for we left our new-found home.
But in spirit our new family would now help us to press on.

4. We face trials, imperfection; there is much now to resist.
But together we are steadfast; all together we persist.

*Refrain:*
We are rising up together in a circle side by side.
Let us learn to love each other, so it may grow deep and wide.

Words: McKenzie Brown
Music: Charles H. Gabriel
Words © 2018 McKenzie Brown.

UNBROKEN CIRCLE
8.7.8.7 with refrain

# We Celebrate Her Many Names  65

*Genesis 1:1-2, 49:25; Exodus 29:45, 40:34-38; Proverbs 1:20-23, 3:13-18;*
*Isaiah 66:13; John 15:15; 1 Corinthians 1:24*

1. We celebrate Her many names: Sophia, Hokmah, Wisdom, Shekhinah, Ruah, El Shaddai; Her names bring truth and freedom. Too long Her names have been ignored, excluded, stifled, unexplored, though found in Holy Scripture.
2. We celebrate Her many names: the Source of all creation, Our Loving Mother, Sister Friend; Her names bring transformation. Oh, how we need Her healing care, Her peace and justice everywhere, so everyone can flourish.
3. We celebrate Her many names, and spread Her ancient story, Her liberating acts and words, Her wondrous grace and glory. We praise Her many holy names, Her sacred power to reclaim, within us ever growing.

Words: Jann Aldredge-Clanton
Music: attr. Nicolaus Decius
Words © 2020 Jann Aldredge-Clanton.

ALLEIN GOTT IN DER HÖH
8.7.8.7.8.8.7

# 66 We Searched Many Years for a Spiritual Home

*Proverbs 1:20-23; Acts 2:17*

1. We searched many years for a spiritual home, a place where all talents can shine; then we heard Her strong voice, and we made a clear choice to follow the Female Divine.
2. Excluded in language and leadership too, we often gave up on our quest; then we made a new place where each gender and race is equally valued and blessed.
3. We move ever forward to open each door, affirming and welcoming all, and at last we can grow in Her life-giving flow; together we follow Her call.

Words: Jann Aldredge-Clanton
Music: George D. Moore
Words © 2019 Jann Aldredge-Clanton.

HAVEN OF REST
11.8.12.8 with refrain

# We Will Unite

68

*Amos 5:24; Ephesians 4:3-4*

1. We will u-nite to la-bor for jus-tice, filled with the Spir-it's power, ris-ing to-geth-er, call-ing for ac-tion, claim-ing Her strength each hour.
2. We will u-nite to chal-lenge a-bus-es, moved by the Spir-it's call, rais-ing our voic-es, tell-ing our sto-ries, break-ing di-vid-ing walls.
3. We will u-nite on path-ways of heal-ing, stirred by the Spir-it's voice, bridg-ing di-vi-sions, work-ing to-geth-er for e-qual rights and choice.

She will give us pow-er, pow-er and lib-er-ty; join-ing Her on mis-sion, we will all be free.
She will give us power and lib-er-ty; join-ing Her, with

Words: Jann Aldredge-Clanton
Music: James H. Fillmore
Words © 2019 Jann Aldredge-Clanton.

RESOLUTION
10.6.10.6 with refrain

# 69 We're Not Alone

1. Through sleepless nights, so often we wonder: Why does such sadness seem to pervade? Why do our minds at times seem to fight us, making us fear the start of each day?
2. Sometimes I wonder why we must suffer through toxic thoughts we can't seem to quell; racing, they make our spirits so restless, longing for when all things shall be well.
3. Mother, please walk with us through this journey; we are unsteady, we feel alone; help us to find You deep in the valley; help us to make this valley a home.

Words: McKenzie Brown
Music: W. B. Stevens
Words © 2019 McKenzie Brown.

FARTHER ALONG
10.9.10.9 with refrain

# 70 When We Are Struggling with Doubt and Fear

*Genesis 1:1-2; John 14:17*

1. When we are struggling with doubt and fear,
   come, Ruah* Spirit, strengthen our souls;
   fill us with courage to persevere,
   working for freedom from stifling roles.

2. Now we see wisdom and truth denied,
   honesty threatened, justice erased;
   come to us, Ruah, to heal and guide;
   bring Your amazing, transforming grace.

3. Come to us, Spirit of truth and life;
   stir us with hope and visions anew,
   dreams of a world where all people thrive,
   joined in creating a peaceful view.

Words: Jann Aldredge-Clanton
Music: Daniel B. Towner
Words © 2020 Jann Aldredge-Clanton.

MOODY
9.9.9.9 with refrain

*Ruah is the word for "Spirit" in the Hebrew Scriptures.

# 71. When We Rise Up All Together
*Deuteronomy 32:11-12*

1. We are tired of in-e-qual-i-ty, a-buse and vio-lence too; we re-fuse to sit in si-lence an-y-more. We will raise our voic-es, speak-ing out for chang-es o-ver-due; we are ris-ing all to-geth-er; hear us roar. When we
2. In our jus-tice work we of-ten feel dis-tressed and o-ver-whelmed, and it's hard to find the strength to car-ry on. Then our Moth-er Ea-gle takes us up to glimpse a bright-er realm, as we rise with Her a-gain to face the dawn. When we
3. We will soar with Moth-er Ea-gle as our en-er-gy re-news; Her sup-port and lov-ing care will nev-er cease. She will lift us up to-geth-er to be-hold a glo-rious view; now the morn-ing breaks with ev-er-last-ing peace.

Words: Jann Aldredge-Clanton
Music: James M. Black
Words © 2018 Jann Aldredge-Clanton.

ROLL CALL
15.11.15.11 with refrain

*Small notes (stems down) are for keyboard accompaniment.
**Small notes (stems up) are for optional vocal harmony.

# 73. Wisdom Sophia Is Calling
*Proverbs 1:20-21, 3:16-18*

1. Wisdom Sophia is calling, through the confusion and noise;
now in the chaos around us, we hear Her comforting voice.
2. Wisdom Sophia is healing, sharing the burdens we bear;
even through all of our struggles, we feel Her tenderest care.
3. Wisdom Sophia is birthing, bringing new life to the earth;
joining with Her in creating, we feel our power and worth.

*Refrain:*
Wisdom is calling, longing to free us from fear;
She gives us hope through each challenge, holding us always near.

Words: Jann Aldredge-Clanton
Music: James McGranahan
Words © 2020 Jann Aldredge-Clanton.

SHOWERS OF BLESSING
8.7.8.7 with refrain

# Wisdom Sophia Keeps Giving
74

*Proverbs 3:13-18; Micah 6:8*

1. When our path-way is hard and lone-ly, and the drear-y days seem so long,
2. When our work for re-form is sti-fled, and we won-der if peo-ple care,
3. When we fol-low Her paths of jus-tice, and we join in Her work of peace,

then So-phi-a will come to strength-en our hearts with hope-ful songs.
then So-phi-a will give us cour-age and free-dom songs to share.
then So-phi-a will fill our spir-its with songs that nev-er cease.

Wis-dom So-phi-a keeps giv-ing lib-er-at-ing, em-pow-er-ing songs, new songs to up-lift us on jour-neys so long; She em-pow-ers our spir-its with songs.

Words: Jann Aldredge-Clanton
Music: Earnest O. Sellers
Words © 2019 Jann Aldredge-Clanton.

NEW ORLEANS
9.8.9.6 with refrain

# NOTES ON THE SONGS

2.       **Circles of Freedom**
16.     **Gather Everywhere in Circles**

The inspiration for these songs came from Ann Smith and from New Wineskins Community. In *She Lives! Sophia Wisdom Works in the World*, I included a profile of Ann, co-founder and director of Circle Connections and co-founder of "Millionth Circle." It has been my joy to participate in sacred circles that Ann facilitated at the Parliament of the World's Religions in Salt Lake City, the UN Commission on the Status of Women in New York City, and the Cathedral of St. John Divine, where she also joined a panel presentation of *She Lives!* With her deep belief in the transformative power of sacred circles, Ann has been for many years what she calls a "circle evangelist," spreading circles throughout the world through her facilitation of circles and circle training workshops, as well as her website and blog. For more than twenty-six years New Wineskins Community in Dallas, Texas, has been practicing circle principles through our shared leadership and empowerment of everyone's gifts. We join together in a circle for our rituals that name and image the Divine as female and male and more to support the equality and value of all. We claim our shared power and responsibility to change culture from patriarchal to egalitarian. Our mission is to expand experience of Divine Mystery and to contribute to healing, equity, justice, and peace in our community, our country, and our world. New Wineskins Community joins other liberating, empowering circles everywhere to transform the world.


3.       **Come and See a Revelation**

The inspiration for this song came from a sermon Rev. Dr. Irie Lynne Session preached at The Gathering, A Womanist Church in January of 2019. The title of her sermon was "No Longer Thirsty," based on the story of the Samaritan woman (John 4:7-42). She interpreted this text from the womanist framework of intersectionality of race, gender, sexuality, class, and patriarchal oppression. As a ministry partner of The Gathering, I join in the womanist mission of dismantling racism, patriarchy, misogyny, and sexism. Rev. Dr. Irie and the other co-pastor of The Gathering, Rev. Kamilah Hall Sharp, often invite me to write and lead litanies for worship services. The litany I wrote for this service in January of 2019 connected the story of the Samaritan woman with the Epiphany season. After this service I wrote "Come and See a Revelation," inspired by Rev. Dr. Irie's sermon and Epiphany.

4. **Come and Seek Sophia Wisdom**

19. **Hear Her Urgent Cry**

47. **She Calls Everyone**

48. **She Will Heal Us**

56. **Spirit of Love**

These songs reclaim some of my favorite "invitation" gospel tunes. In the Baptist church where I grew up, an invitation concluded every worship service. The congregation sang a hymn while the pastor extended the invitation and stood at the front of the church to receive people who walked down the aisle. This invitation emphasized personal salvation through belief in Jesus and his blood atonement. My songs to these tunes instead invite everyone to answer *Sophia* Wisdom's call to follow Her in bringing justice, healing, love, peace, and transformation in the world.

5. **Come, El Shaddai, with Tender Care**

44. **Rise Up Together Now**

In the midst of the global coronavirus pandemic in the summer of 2020, wildfires devastated large areas in California and Oregon, and in October of the same year hurricanes caused widespread destruction in Louisiana. These environmental disasters and the pandemic took the heaviest toll on communities of color. I wrote "Come, El Shaddai, with Tender Care" as a prayer for peace, healing, and tender care for all those going through the "floods and flames" and to those suffering distress, pain, and grief from the pandemic. "Rise Up Together Now" is a call to claim the Spirit's power for rising in partnership to resist environmental injustice and all forms of injustice.

## 9. Come Quickly, Sophia

Between 2017 and 2018 the US government separated more than 5000 children from their parents at the US-Mexico border. Many of these children, detained in chain-link cages, suffered from various kinds of abuse, including unhygienic conditions, poor nourishment, inadequate emotional care, and lack of health care. As of fall 2020, parents of 545 children separated at the border still could not be found. This song came from my distress over the injustices these children and parents suffered, and the refusal of the administration at that time to tell the truth about them. The song is a prayer to *Sophia* Wisdom to show us Her way to help set these captives free.

## 10, 10a.   Come Together, Celebrate

This song was commissioned by Pullen Memorial Baptist Church to celebrate Larry E. Schultz on the occasion of his 20th anniversary in ministry with the church. The song celebrates his music ministry as a talented conductor, composer, educator, and prophetic minister. I wrote these lyrics also in appreciation of my collaboration with Larry for 20 years. The reference to "Sister-Brother Spirit" in stanza two is a divine image that Larry and I have seen as guiding our creative partnership. It has been a joy to collaborate with Larry on five hymn collections, a children's musical, a children's song and activity book, and anthems for children and adults. Larry composed the tune SPIRIT DANCE for one of our first collaborations. This joyful, soaring tune aptly expresses the lyrics I wrote for "Come Together, Celebrate." Also, I chose the tune HYMN TO JOY for the celebratory words of "Come, Together, Celebrate."

The version of the song in this collection substitutes plural pronouns for the singular masculine pronouns referring to Larry in the original version. This plural version celebrates ministers of music in general, but can also be used as a nonbinary reference to an individual minister of music. The pronouns "he" or "she" can also be used to refer to a specific minister of music.

## 11. Creative Darkness Fills the Earth

## 46. Sacred Darkness, Deep Within Us

These songs change the traditional negative symbolism of darkness to positive images of darkness as creative, sacred, miraculous, powerful, and life-giving. These positive images of darkness in worship emphasize the sacred value of people of color, who too often are devalued and oppressed. These songs also call everyone to claim the "wondrous miracles," "hidden treasures," and "rich abundance" of darkness to deepen our spiritual experience and work toward the Beloved Community of inclusiveness, social justice, equity, love, and peace.

## 12. El Shaddai

## 15. Friend of All

These songs are dedicated in loving memory to my father, Truman Aldredge, a pastor and lover of music. He had a beautiful baritone voice, and would often break out into singing in the midst or end of sermons and at home. Two of his favorite gospel songs were "Stand by Me" and "No, Not One." I can still hear his deep resonant voice singing "When the storms of life are raging, stand by me" and "There's not a friend like the lowly Jesus, no, not one." In the 1950s and 1960s in a small town in Louisiana, he preached prophetic sermons on race in spite of much criticism from the church. He almost lost his position as pastor of First Baptist Church in Minden, Louisiana, because of his courageous stands. Because he experienced the "storms of life" and loss of friends, these songs touched his spirit. Although the original words are still meaningful to me, I felt inspired to write new lyrics that reimagine the Divine Female as Friend, Comforter, and Healer. Also, I remember his preaching a sermon series on the many names of the Divine, including *El Shaddai*. He died many years before I became an ordained pastor and began writing on gender equality and expansive names and images of the Divine. But just as he was prophetic on race, I believe he celebrates my pastoral ministry and that of other women, as well as the inclusion of the Divine Female in liturgy.

**13. Ever Embracing ∞ Ever Becoming**

**42. Pillar of Salt**

**54. Spirit of Godde, Spark of Creation**

**61. They Who Wait**

**72. Who Will Bring Relief?**

Larry E. Schultz wrote the words and music for these congregational songs. In his 20th year as minister of music at Pullen Memorial Baptist Church in Raleigh, North Carolina, Larry wrote "Ever Embracing ∞ Ever Becoming" in gratitude to Roger Crook and Robert McMillan for conveying the heritage and inspiring the hope of the church. The phrases "Ever Embracing" and "Ever Becoming," along with the infinity symbol in the center, are from two art panels in the sanctuary. Since its beginning as a ministry to the disenfranchised, Pullen has been "Ever Embracing" and has also been "Ever Becoming," always evolving. "Pillar of Salt," inspired by Hebrew Biblical Scholar Brian Crisp (for whom the tune is named), asks this thought-provoking question and transforms our thinking about a derided biblical figure: What if, instead of fleeing from a city in devastation without concern, Lot's wife turns in compassion to view and reach out to humanity (and perhaps other left-behind daughters, family and friends)? Then her act becomes one of selfless strength, immortalized in the image of a pillar of salt, and an example for all. "Spirit of Godde, Spark of Creation" expresses various metaphorical descriptions for the Spirit as found in ancient Hebrew/Christian tradition and also contemporary life. It is meaningfully used at Pentecost or any time of year. "They Who Wait," based on Isaiah 40:31, encourages patient waiting for future strength. Larry composed this song during the pandemic in 2021, and it is meaningful during any season when days are long. "Who Will Bring Relief?" offers a contemplation and response to the passage from Isaiah's scroll (Isaiah 61:1) read by Jesus in his hometown synagogue (Luke 4:18).

**14. Every Moment the Divine Gives Life**

My references to "all genders" and "every gender" in many of my songs in this and previous collections indicate my reaching beyond the gender binary classification of two distinct, opposite forms of masculine and feminine. Larry Schultz encouraged me to write a song referring to the Divine as "they" as another way of including nonbinary persons. The word "they" is now widely accepted as a singular, as well as plural, gender nonbinary pronoun, and many people request references to themselves as "they." I use "they" in this song as both singular and plural to refer to the Divine. The singular reference celebrates the sacred image in a nonbinary person who goes by "they," and the plural reference emphasizes the multiplicity of Divinity, also making this song appropriate for multifaith settings.

**24. In These Times of Deep Division**

This song, written in the midst of primaries preceding the 2020 presidential election, acknowledges the deep political and ideological divisions in our country, and the systemic injustices that keep us bound. This song, like many others in this collection, highlights the long-ignored biblical female divine image of Holy Wisdom, who brings healing and peace (Proverbs 3:17-18). We sing of joining Holy Wisdom in Her work of justice, peace, equity, grace, love, and new life.

26. Join to Create

36. O Mother Godde

37. O Mother Godde, I Come

60. There's Justice Work for Us to Do

62. We Are Building on Her Love Eternal

64. We Are Rising Up Together

67. We Must Follow Her Way

69. We're Not Alone

McKenzie Brown, a composer and lyricist, contributed these songs to this collection. Soon after we began our collaboration, she wrote the lyrics for the song "We Are Rising Up Together" to the gospel tune UNBROKEN CIRCLE. This song came from her joy in finding community in a Christian Feminism Today Gathering, where for the first time she had experienced female divine names and images in worship. McKenzie sang "We Are Rising Up Together" at the national Nevertheless She Preached 2018 Conference in Waco, Texas, and it has become a favorite of New Wineskins Community in Dallas. McKenzie went on to write the lyrics for "O Mother Godde, I Come," "There's Justice Work for Us to Do," "We Must Follow Her Way," and "We're Not Alone," and to collaborate with me on "Join to Create" "O Mother Godde," and "We Are Building on Her Love Eternal."

## 27. Keeping Hope Alive

For more than thirty years I have researched, preached, taught, and written books on the importance of including biblical female names and images of the Divine in our worship if we are to have social justice and equity. Others have advocated for inclusive language and theology even longer. Meeting resistance and indifference, we often struggle to keep our hope for change alive. This song expresses feelings of weariness and discouragement as we pray for faith and strength to continue doing this justice work. The song concludes with the hope and healing we find in new communities who support equity by including female divine names and images—communities such as New Wineskins Community; Ebenezer/herchurch Lutheran; Equity for Women in the Church; The Gathering, A Womanist Church; Christian Feminism Today; Women's Alliance for Theology, Ethics, and Ritual (WATER); and The Association of Roman Catholic Women Priests.

**28. Liberating Christ-Sophia**

**35. Now Her Voice Liberates**

**43. Power in Us All**

**51. Sister-Brother Spirit Sets Us Free**

**52. So Many People Cry in Pain**

**58. The Power of Love**

These songs reclaim some of my favorite gospel tunes that I can no longer sing with the original words because of their emphasis on blood redemption. I had planned to use them in a workshop that John Ballenger invited me to co-lead with him at the annual Alliance of Baptists Gathering, scheduled for April of 2020. The topic of our workshop was hymnody and liturgy on the theme of atonement for progressive churches. John and I began planning our workshop in May of 2019, and I sent him "The Power of Love," "So Many People Cry in Pain," and "Power in Us All." John wrote back with affirmation and gratitude for these new lyrics. In March of 2020, the Alliance leaders made the wise decision to postpone the Gathering because of the pandemic. I kept writing new lyrics that reimagine the atonement from a progressive Christian viewpoint for the workshop, rescheduled for the 2022 Gathering.

**31. Loving Shepherd Comes to Guide Us**

**32. Loving Shepherd Calls**

These songs are dedicated in loving memory to my mother, Eva Louise Hickerson Aldredge Henley. Bobby McFerrin's references to the Shepherd as "She" in his song "The 23rd Psalm" reminded me that shepherds are female, as well as male, even though most biblical translations of Psalm 23 use masculine pronouns to refer to the Shepherd. Feminine pronouns illuminate the comforting and empowering images of the psalm in fresh ways. My mother was a shepherd to many people, especially to people in the "Any and All" Sunday school class she taught for 35 years in San Angelo, Texas. She welcomed everyone to her class that included five races and various ages, genders, and economic backgrounds. Although never a pastor because of restrictions placed on women in her Baptist tradition, she had pastoral gifts that made her just as qualified as my father to shepherd a church. In her role as pastor's wife in four churches, she served as an unpaid, untitled shepherd to a wide diversity of people. These lines in "Loving Shepherd Comes to Guide Us" describe her ministry: "All genders and all races will find a welcome place in her expansive, liberating home." One of my mother's favorite hymns was "Jesus Paid It All." The original words with blood atonement theology no longer have meaning for me. So in "Loving Shepherd Calls," I reclaim this beautiful tune with images of the Shepherd in Luke 15, who guides us and comes with tender care "when we're lost and all alone."

**34. New Life Awaits Us All**

One of my fondest memories of visits to my paternal grandparents' home in Abilene, Texas, is playing the piano for family members gathered around to sing gospel hymns. I can still hear Aunt Lavelle, Aunt Katie, Aunt Polly, Aunt Betty, Uncle Leland, my granddad, and my dad singing in beautiful harmony. Their favorite hymns envisioned the glories of heaven. When McKenzie and I were looking for gospel tunes for this collection, we found that many focus on the afterlife, and we wrote lyrics to some of these tunes such as UNBROKEN CIRCLE, THE UNCLOUDED DAY, SWEET BY AND BY, and ROLL CALL.

I chose the lilting tune THIS WORLD IS NOT MY HOME for my song "New Life Awaits Us All." The original words rejoice in the angels' beckoning "from heaven's open door." My lyrics celebrate open doors and transformation in this life and the life beyond: "She calls us always forward through the open doors, and we keep on embracing new life evermore."

## 41. Our Sister Spirit

The inspiration for this song came from my participation as a ministry partnern The Gathering, A Womanist Church, where I find the Divine embodied in Black women who preach prophetic sermons and in those who sing freedom songs. Many Black women experience the triple oppression of racism, sexism, and classism. The Gathering embraces womanist theology that centers the experiences of Black women while working for the survival and wholeness of all people and all creation. "Our Sister Spirit" expresses the truth of the Divine incarnated in others who are oppressed and devalued (Matthew 25:35-40), naming children who have been separated from their parents at the US-Mexico border, factory workers who suffer from poor wages and conditions, and the elderly who are too often ignored.

## 45. Ruah Spirit Calls Within

At the 2019 Hymn Society Annual Conference in Dallas, Texas, I attended a text writers' workshop. David Gambrell, Associate for Worship in the Presbyterian Church (U.S.A.) Office of Theology and award-winning hymn writer, faciliated this workshop and led the discussion of hymns submitted before the conference, including "Ruah Spirit Calls Within." Gambrell and others in the workshop expressed appreciation for the biblical female divine name *Ruah* and female pronouns in my hymn, commenting on the need for more female divine names and images in hymnody. His helpful suggestions and those of others in the workshop contributed to this hymn.

### 65. We Celebrate Her Many Names

This song includes some of the biblical female names for the Divine I have discovered through many years of research and writing. It also laments that Her names have for too long been "ignored, excluded, stifled, unexplored" by churches even though found in the Bible that they exalt. "We Celebrate Her Many Names" also expresses longing for the healing, transformation, liberation, peace, and justice She brings "so everyone can flourish."

### 66. We Searched Many Years for a Spiritual Home

Many people have searched for a long time for a church home where all genders and races are included and given equal value through worship language and leadership. In 1989 in Waco, Texas, I joined a diverse group who had grown tired of the resistance to inclusive language in churches, so we formed The Inclusive Worship Community, committed to gender and racial inclusiveness. In 1995 in Dallas, I also met people who had searched for many years but couldn't find a racially diverse spiritual home where female names and images of the Divine and women leaders were included, so we created New Wineskins Community. McKenzie later searched and found New Wineskins Community. We both also found an inclusive spiritual home in Christian Feminism Today. I wrote "We Searched Many Years for a Spiritual Home" in celebration of these communities and of other inclusive faith communities where "at last we can grow in Her life-giving flow": Ebenezer/herchurch Lutheran in San Francisco; Equity for Women in the Church; The Gathering, A Womanist Church in Dallas; Women's Alliance for Theology, Ethics, and Ritual (WATER); and The Association of Roman Catholic Women Priests.

### 74. Wisdom Sophia Keeps Giving

The inspiration for this song came while I was walking, filled with gratitude for the new lyrics Wisdom *Sophia* continued to give McKenzie and me for this collection. When I was growing up, one of my favorite gospel songs was "Wonderful, Wonderful Jesus," which expresses the power of songs to give us courage and strength through burdensome days. "Wisdom Sophia Keeps Giving" to this same tune celebrates Her coming through difficult and discouraging times with gifts of hopeful, empowering, liberating new songs to uplift our spirits.

# TOPICAL INDEX OF SONGS

### ADVERSITY

| | |
|---|---|
| Come Quickly, Sophia | 9 |
| Holy Wisdom Fills Our Hearts with Song | 22 |
| O Mother Godde | 36 |
| Pillar of Salt | 42 |
| They Who Wait | 61 |
| When We Rise Up All Together | 71 |
| Who Will Bring Relief? | 72 |

### BEAUTY

| | |
|---|---|
| Come Together, Celebrate | 10, 10a |
| Creative Darkness Fills the Earth | 11 |
| Liberating Christ-Sophia | 28 |
| Sacred Darkness, Deep Within Us | 46 |
| Spirit of Godde, Spark of Creation | 54 |
| We Celebrate Her Many Names | 65 |

### CALL

| | |
|---|---|
| Come, El Shaddai, with Tender Care | 5 |
| Come Together, Celebrate | 10, 10a |
| Creative Darkness Fills the Earth | 11 |
| Friend of All | 15 |
| Hokmah Wisdom Shows the Way | 20 |
| Holy Wisdom Calls | 21 |
| Holy Wisdom Fills Our Hearts with Song | 22 |
| In These Times of Deep Division | 24 |
| Liberating Spirit Calls | 29 |
| Longing for Healing Peace | 30 |
| Loving Shepherd Calls | 32 |
| Now Her Voice Liberates | 35 |
| Our Mother Inspires All Our Work | 39 |

Ruah Spirit Calls Within..................................................................................45
She Calls Everyone ......................................................................................47
Spirit of Godde, Spark of Creation..............................................................54
The Spirit of Life..........................................................................................59
We Searched Many Years for a Spiritual Home .........................................66
We Will Unite..............................................................................................68
Who Will Bring Relief?................................................................................72
Wisdom Sophia Is Calling...........................................................................73

## CARE OF CREATION (see also Earth Day)

Circles of Freedom........................................................................................2
Come, Holy Spirit, Bring Your Vision..........................................................7
Creative Darkness Fills the Earth...............................................................11
Liberating Christ-Sophia............................................................................28
Loving Shepherd Comes to Guide Us .......................................................31
Our Mother Inspires All Our Work...........................................................39
Rise Up Together Now................................................................................44
Ruah Spirit Calls Within............................................................................45
Sacred Darkness Deep Within Us..............................................................46
She Calls Everyone .....................................................................................47
Shekhinah Is Shining on Earth..................................................................49
Spirit of Life and Love................................................................................55
Spirit of Love...............................................................................................56
Spirit of Power............................................................................................57
The Power of Love .....................................................................................58
We Are Building on Her Love Eternal......................................................62
Wisdom Sophia Is Calling..........................................................................73

## CELEBRATION

Come, Give Us Power for Our Day..............................................................6
Come Together, Celebrate ................................................................. 10, 10a
Ever Embracing ∞ Ever Becoming.............................................................13
Join to Create..............................................................................................26
Loving Shepherd Calls................................................................................32
O Mother Godde ........................................................................................36
We Celebrate Her Many Names.................................................................65

**CHALLENGE**

Circles of Freedom ......................................................................................... 2
Ever Embracing ∞ Ever Becoming ................................................................ 13
Keeping Hope Alive ........................................................................................ 27
O Mother Godde ............................................................................................ 36
Pillar of Salt .................................................................................................... 42
They Who Wait ............................................................................................... 61
We Are Rising Up Together ............................................................................ 64
When We Rise Up All Together ..................................................................... 71
Who Will Bring Relief? .................................................................................. 72
Wisdom Sophia Is Calling .............................................................................. 73

**COMFORT**

Come, El Shaddai, with Tender Care ............................................................... 5
Loving Shepherd Comes to Guide Us ............................................................ 31
O Mother Godde, I Come .............................................................................. 37
Spirit of Godde, Spark of Creation ................................................................ 54
Spirit of Love ................................................................................................. 56
We're Not Alone ............................................................................................. 69
Wisdom Sophia Is Calling .............................................................................. 73

**COMMUNITY**

Circles of Freedom ......................................................................................... 2
Come Now, All-Inclusive Spirit ....................................................................... 8
Come Together, Celebrate ..................................................................... 10, 10a
Creative Darkness Fills the Earth .................................................................. 11
Ever Embracing ∞ Ever Becoming ................................................................ 13
Gather Everywhere in Circles ........................................................................ 16
Guiding on Healing Paths .............................................................................. 18
Hear Her Urgent Cry ...................................................................................... 19
Holy Wisdom Fills Our Hearts with Song ..................................................... 22
Join All Together As One ............................................................................... 25
Join to Create ................................................................................................. 26
Keeping Hope Alive ....................................................................................... 27
Move Throughout Our World Today ............................................................. 33

Rise Up Together Now ......................................................................... 44
Ruah Spirit Calls Within ...................................................................... 45
Sacred Darkness, Deep Within Us ..................................................... 46
We Are Rising Up Together ................................................................ 64
We Searched Many Years for a Spiritual Home ............................... 66
When We Rise Up All Together .......................................................... 71

## COURAGE

Christ-Sophia, Give Us Wisdom ........................................................... 1
Circles of Freedom .................................................................................. 2
Guiding on Healing Paths ................................................................... 18
Join All Together As One ..................................................................... 25
Liberating Christ-Sophia ..................................................................... 28
Liberating Spirit Calls ......................................................................... 29
Our Mother Inspires All Our Work ................................................... 39
Pillar of Salt .......................................................................................... 42
Sacred Darkness, Deep Within Us ..................................................... 46
Sister Spirit Shows the Healing Way ................................................. 50
The Spirit of Life .................................................................................. 59
They Who Wait ..................................................................................... 61
When We Are Struggling with Doubt and Fear ............................... 70
When We Rise Up All Together .......................................................... 71
Wisdom Sophia Keeps Giving ............................................................ 74

## CREATION

Circles of Freedom .................................................................................. 2
Come, Holy Spirit, Bring Your Vision .................................................. 7
El Shaddai .............................................................................................. 12
Every Moment the Divine Gives Life ................................................. 14
Liberating Spirit Calls ......................................................................... 29
Loving Shepherd Comes to Guide Us ............................................... 31
Our Mother Inspires All Our Work ................................................... 39
Ruah Spirit Calls Within ...................................................................... 45
Sacred Darkness Deep Within Us ...................................................... 46
She Calls Everyone ............................................................................... 47

Shekhinah Is Shining on Earth..................................................................49
Spirit of Godde, Spark of Creation............................................................54
Spirit of Love..............................................................................................56
The Power of Love.....................................................................................58
We Are Building on Her Love Eternal......................................................62

## CREATIVITY

Come, Give Us Power for Our Day...............................................................6
Come, Holy Spirit, Bring Your Vision...........................................................7
Come Together, Celebrate................................................................. 10, 10a
Every Moment the Divine Gives Life..........................................................14
Gather Everywhere in Circles.....................................................................16
Great Is Sophia............................................................................................17
Hokmah Wisdom Shows the Way..............................................................20
Holy Wisdom Fills Our Hearts with Song..................................................22
Join to Create...............................................................................................26
Move Throughout Our World Today..........................................................33
Sacred Darkness, Deep Within Us..............................................................46
Wisdom Sophia Is Calling..........................................................................73

## DIVINE IMAGES

**Advocate**
  Our Loving Mother................................................................................40
**All-Inclusive Spirit**
  Come Now, All-Inclusive Spirit...............................................................8
**Breath of Life**
  Move Throughout Our World Today....................................................33
**Brother Spirit**
  On Our Journey.....................................................................................38
**Christ-Sophia**
  Christ-Sophia, Give Us Wisdom.............................................................1
  Come, Give Us Power for Our Day........................................................6
  Liberating Christ-Sophia......................................................................28
**Creative Darkness**
  Creative Darkness Fills the Earth..........................................................11

**Divine**
    Every Moment the Divine Gives Life ............................................................. 14
**El Shaddai**
    Come, El Shaddai, with Tender Care ............................................................... 5
    El Shaddai ............................................................................................................. 12
    We Celebrate Her Many Names ....................................................................... 65
**Faithful Friend**
    Loving Shepherd Comes to Guide Us ............................................................ 31
**Female Divine**
    We Searched Many Years for a Spiritual Home ........................................... 66
**Friend**
    El Shaddai ............................................................................................................. 12
    Friend of All ......................................................................................................... 15
    Loving Shepherd Comes to Guide Us ............................................................ 31
    We Celebrate Her Many Names ....................................................................... 65
**Godde**
    Keeping Hope Alive ........................................................................................... 27
    O Mother Godde .................................................................................................. 36
    O Mother Godde, I Come .................................................................................. 37
    Spirit of Godde, Spark of Creation .................................................................. 54
**Giver**
    El Shaddai ............................................................................................................. 12
**Ground**
    Our Loving Mother ............................................................................................ 40
**Guide**
    In These Times of Deep Division ..................................................................... 24
**Healing Wind**
    Move Throughout Our World Today .............................................................. 33
**Heavenly Dove**
    Come Together, Celebrate ........................................................................ 10, 10a
    She Will Heal Us ................................................................................................. 48
**Hokmah**
    Hokmah Wisdom Shows the Way ................................................................... 20
    We Celebrate Her Many Names ....................................................................... 65
**Holy Spirit**
    Come, Holy Spirit, Bring Your Vision .............................................................. 7
**Holy Wisdom**
    Holy Wisdom Calls ............................................................................................ 21

| | |
|---|---|
| Holy Wisdom Fills Our Hearts with Song | 22 |
| In These Times of Deep Division | 24 |
| Now Her Voice Liberates | 35 |

**Liberating Spirit**
| | |
|---|---|
| Come Together, Celebrate | 10, 10a |
| Liberating Spirit Calls | 29 |

**Life**
| | |
|---|---|
| In These Times of Deep Division | 24 |

**Living Water**
| | |
|---|---|
| Come and See a Revelation | 3 |

**Living Word**
| | |
|---|---|
| Come and See a Revelation | 3 |

**Love**
| | |
|---|---|
| In These Times of Deep Division | 24 |
| The Power of Love | 58 |
| We Are Building on Her Love Eternal | 62 |

**Loving Mother**
| | |
|---|---|
| Our Loving Mother | 40 |
| We Celebrate Her Many Names | 65 |

**Loving Shepherd**
| | |
|---|---|
| Loving Shepherd Calls | 32 |
| Loving Shepherd Comes to Guide Us | 31 |

**Mother**
| | |
|---|---|
| El Shaddai | 12 |
| Keeping Hope Alive | 27 |
| O Mother Godde | 36 |
| O Mother Godde, I Come | 37 |
| Our Loving Mother | 40 |
| Our Mother Inspires All Our Work | 39 |
| There's Justice Work for Us to Do | 60 |
| We Celebrate Her Many Names | 65 |
| We Must Follow Her Way | 67 |
| We're Not Alone | 69 |

**Mother Eagle**
| | |
|---|---|
| In Her Power We Are Rising | 23 |
| When We Rise Up All Together | 71 |

**Mother Godde**
| | |
|---|---|
| Keeping Hope Alive | 27 |

    O Mother Godde ............................................................................... 36
    O Mother Godde, I Come .................................................................. 37
**Mystery**
    Come and See a Revelation ................................................................ 3
**Presence**
    Guiding on Healing Paths ................................................................ 18
**Refuge**
    Loving Shepherd Comes to Guide Us ............................................ 31
**Rock**
    Our Loving Mother ........................................................................... 40
**Ruah**
    Move Throughout Our World Today ............................................ 33
    Ruah Spirit Calls Within .................................................................. 45
    We Are Building on Her Love Eternal .......................................... 62
    We Celebrate Her Many Names ..................................................... 65
    When We Are Struggling with Doubt and Fear ......................... 70
**Sacred Darkness**
    Sacred Darkness, Deep Within Us ................................................ 46
**Shekhinah**
    Guiding on Healing Paths ................................................................ 18
    Shekhinah Is Shining on Earth ....................................................... 49
    We Celebrate Her Many Names ..................................................... 65
**Shepherd**
    Loving Shepherd Calls ..................................................................... 32
    Loving Shepherd Comes to Guide Us ............................................ 31
**Sister-Brother Spirit**
    Sister-Brother Spirit Sets Us Free .................................................. 51
**Sister Friend**
    We Celebrate Her Many Names ..................................................... 65
**Sister Spirit**
    On Our Journey ................................................................................. 38
    Our Sister Spirit ................................................................................. 41
    Sister Spirit Shows the Healing Way ............................................ 50
**Sophia**
    Come and Seek Sophia Wisdom ...................................................... 4
    Come Quickly, Sophia ....................................................................... 9
    Great Is Sophia ................................................................................... 17
    She Calls Everyone ............................................................................ 47

    Sophia Wisdom Gives Us Power .................................................................... 53
    We Celebrate Her Many Names .................................................................... 65
    Wisdom Sophia Is Calling ............................................................................... 73
    Wisdom Sophia Keeps Giving ........................................................................ 74

**Source**
    El Shaddai ........................................................................................................ 12
    In These Times of Deep Division ................................................................... 24
    Spirit of Life and Love .................................................................................... 55
    We Celebrate Her Many Names .................................................................... 65

**Source of Creation**
    Spirit of Power ................................................................................................ 57

**Spirit**
    Circles of Freedom ........................................................................................... 2
    Come, Holy Spirit, Bring Your Vision ............................................................. 7
    Come Together, Celebrate ..................................................................... 10, 10a
    Gather Everywhere in Circles ........................................................................ 16
    Join All Together As One ................................................................................ 25
    New Life Awaits Us All ................................................................................... 34
    Our Sister Spirit .............................................................................................. 41
    Rise Up Together Now ................................................................................... 44
    Ruah Spirit Calls Within ................................................................................ 45
    She Will Heal Us ............................................................................................. 48
    Sister Spirit Shows the Healing Way ............................................................ 50
    Spirit of Godde, Spark of Creation ................................................................ 54
    Spirit of Life and Love .................................................................................... 55
    Spirit of Love ................................................................................................... 56
    Spirit of Power ................................................................................................ 57
    The Spirit of Life ............................................................................................. 59
    We Are Building on Her Love Eternal .......................................................... 62
    We Are Dreaming of a World ........................................................................ 63
    We Will Unite .................................................................................................. 68
    When We Are Struggling with Doubt and Fear .......................................... 70

**Spirit of Life**
    The Spirit of Life ............................................................................................. 59

**Spirit of Life and Love**
    Spirit of Life and Love .................................................................................... 55

**Spirit of Love**
    Spirit of Love ................................................................................................... 56

**Spirit of Power**
    Spirit of Power ................................................................................................. 57
**Transforming Fire**
    Move Throughout Our World Today .............................................................. 33
**Tree of Life**
    In These Times of Deep Division ..................................................................... 24
**Way**
    In These Times of Deep Division ..................................................................... 24
**Wisdom**
    Come and Seek Sophia Wisdom ........................................................................ 4
    Come Quickly, Sophia ......................................................................................... 9
    Ever Embracing ∞ Ever Becoming .................................................................. 13
    Great Is Sophia .................................................................................................. 17
    Hear Her Urgent Cry ........................................................................................ 19
    Hokmah Wisdom Shows the Way ................................................................... 20
    Holy Wisdom Calls ........................................................................................... 21
    Holy Wisdom Fills Our Hearts with Song ...................................................... 22
    In These Times of Deep Division ..................................................................... 24
    Join to Create .................................................................................................... 26
    Longing for Healing Peace ............................................................................... 30
    Now Her Voice Liberates .................................................................................. 35
    Power in Us All ................................................................................................. 43
    She Calls Everyone ........................................................................................... 47
    So Many People Cry in Pain ............................................................................ 52
    Sophia Wisdom Gives Us Power ...................................................................... 53
    The Power of Love ............................................................................................ 58
    We Celebrate Her Many Names ....................................................................... 65
    Wisdom Sophia Is Calling ................................................................................ 73
    Wisdom Sophia Keeps Giving .......................................................................... 74

## EARTH DAY (see also Care of Creation)

Circles of Freedom ................................................................................................. 2
Come, Holy Spirit, Bring Your Vision ................................................................... 7
Creative Darkness Fills the Earth ......................................................................... 11
Liberating Christ-Sophia ...................................................................................... 28
Our Mother Inspires All Our Work ..................................................................... 39

Rise Up Together Now ..................................................................................44
Ruah Spirit Calls Within.................................................................................45
Sacred Darkness Deep Within Us...................................................................46
She Calls Everyone .........................................................................................47
Shekhinah Is Shining on Earth........................................................................49
Spirit of Life and Love ....................................................................................55
Spirit of Love...................................................................................................56
Spirit of Power ................................................................................................57
The Power of Love ..........................................................................................58
We Are Building on Her Love Eternal............................................................62
Wisdom Sophia Is Calling...............................................................................73

## EPIPHANY

Come and See a Revelation..............................................................................3
Creative Darkness Fills the Earth...................................................................11
Shekhinah Is Shining on Earth........................................................................49
We Are Dreaming of a World .........................................................................63
We Searched Many Years for a Spiritual Home .............................................66

## FAITH AND TRUST

In Her Power We Are Rising..........................................................................23
Keeping Hope Alive........................................................................................27
There's Justice Work for Us to Do..................................................................60
They Who Wait ...............................................................................................61

## FREEDOM (see also Liberaton)

Christ-Sophia, Give Us Wisdom......................................................................1
Circles of Freedom...........................................................................................2
Come and Seek Sophia Wisdom ......................................................................4
Come, Give Us Power for Our Day..................................................................6
Come, Holy Spirit, Bring Your Vision.............................................................7
Come Quickly, Sophia .....................................................................................9
Come Together, Celebrate ..................................................................... 10, 10a
Creative Darkness Fills the Earth...................................................................11

Ever Embracing ∞ Ever Becoming................................................................13
Every Moment the Divine Gives Life........................................................14
Great Is Sophia................................................................................................17
Hear Her Urgent Cry....................................................................................19
Hokmah Wisdom Shows the Way..............................................................20
Holy Wisdom Fills Our Hearts with Song................................................22
In These Times of Deep Division................................................................24
Join All Together As One..............................................................................25
Join to Create..................................................................................................26
Liberating Christ-Sophia..............................................................................28
Liberating Spirit Calls..................................................................................29
Loving Shepherd Comes to Guide Us......................................................31
Move Throughout Our World Today........................................................33
New Life Awaits Us All................................................................................34
Now Her Voice Liberates..............................................................................35
O Mother Godde............................................................................................36
Our Sister Spirit..............................................................................................41
Ruah Spirit Calls Within..............................................................................45
She Calls Everyone........................................................................................47
Sister Spirit Shows the Healing Way........................................................50
Sister-Brother Spirit Sets Us Free..............................................................51
So Many People Cry in Pain......................................................................52
Spirit of Life and Love..................................................................................55
Spirit of Love..................................................................................................56
Spirit of Power................................................................................................57
We Are Building on Her Love Eternal....................................................62
We Are Dreaming of a World....................................................................63
We Celebrate Her Many Names................................................................65
We Will Unite..................................................................................................68
When We Are Struggling with Doubt and Fear....................................70
Who Will Bring Relief?................................................................................72
Wisdom Sophia Keeps Giving....................................................................74

## GIVING AND RECEIVING

Come Together, Celebrate.................................................................. 10, 10a
Creative Darkness Fills the Earth..............................................................11

El Shaddai ..................................................................................................12
Ever Embracing ∞ Ever Becoming.................................................................13
Every Moment the Divine Gives Life..............................................................14
Gather Everywhere in Circles.........................................................................16
Hokmah Wisdom Shows the Way...................................................................20
Liberating Spirit Calls ....................................................................................29
Power in Us All...............................................................................................43
Spirit of Godde, Spark of Creation .................................................................54
We Searched Many Years for a Spiritual Home .............................................66
We're Not Alone .............................................................................................69
Who Will Bring Relief?...................................................................................72
Wisdom Sophia Keeps Giving........................................................................74

## GRACE

Christ-Sophia, Give Us Wisdom.......................................................................1
Come, El Shaddai, with Tender Care................................................................5
Come Now, All-Inclusive Spirit ........................................................................8
Great Is Sophia................................................................................................17
In Her Power We Are Rising...........................................................................23
In These Times of Deep Division ...................................................................24
Join All Together As One ................................................................................25
O Mother Godde, I Come ...............................................................................37
Our Loving Mother ........................................................................................40
Our Mother Inspires All Our Work ................................................................39
She Will Heal Us.............................................................................................48
Spirit of Life and Love ....................................................................................55
The Spirit of Life.............................................................................................59
We Celebrate Her Many Names.....................................................................65
When We Are Struggling with Doubt and Fear ............................................70

## GUIDANCE AND CARE

Christ-Sophia, Give Us Wisdom.......................................................................1
Come, El Shaddai, with Tender Care................................................................5
Come Now, All-Inclusive Spirit ........................................................................8
Come Together, Celebrate ...................................................................... 10, 10a
Creative Darkness Fills the Earth...................................................................11

El Shaddai ........................................................................................................ 12
Guiding on Healing Paths .............................................................................. 18
Hokmah Wisdom Shows the Way .................................................................. 20
Holy Wisdom Calls ......................................................................................... 21
In Her Power We Are Rising .......................................................................... 23
Join to Create .................................................................................................. 26
Liberating Christ-Sophia ................................................................................ 28
Liberating Spirit Calls .................................................................................... 29
Loving Shepherd Calls ................................................................................... 32
Loving Shepherd Comes to Guide Us ........................................................... 31
Move Throughout Our World Today ............................................................ 33
On Our Journey .............................................................................................. 38
Our Loving Mother ........................................................................................ 40
She Calls Everyone ......................................................................................... 47
She Will Heal Us ............................................................................................. 48
Sister-Brother Spirit Sets Us Free .................................................................. 51
Spirit of Godde, Spark of Creation ............................................................... 54
Spirit of Power ................................................................................................ 57
There's Justice Work for Us to Do ................................................................. 60
We Are Building on Her Love Eternal .......................................................... 62
We Are Dreaming of a World ........................................................................ 63
When We Are Struggling with Doubt and Fear .......................................... 70

**HEALING**

Christ-Sophia, Give Us Wisdom ..................................................................... 1
Come and Seek Sophia Wisdom ..................................................................... 4
Come, El Shaddai, with Tender Care ............................................................. 5
Come, Holy Spirit, Bring Your Vision ............................................................ 7
Come Now, All-Inclusive Spirit ...................................................................... 8
Come Quickly, Sophia ..................................................................................... 9
Friend of All ................................................................................................... 15
Gather Everywhere in Circles ....................................................................... 16
Great Is Sophia ............................................................................................... 17
Guiding on Healing Paths ............................................................................. 18
Holy Wisdom Fills Our Hearts with Song ................................................... 22
In These Times of Deep Division .................................................................. 24

Liberating Christ-Sophia ..................................................................28
Liberating Spirit Calls ......................................................................29
Longing for Healing Peace ...............................................................30
Loving Shepherd Comes to Guide Us ..............................................31
Move Throughout Our World Today ...............................................33
Now Her Voice Liberates ..................................................................35
On Our Journey ................................................................................38
Our Loving Mother ..........................................................................40
Ruah Spirit Calls Within ..................................................................45
She Calls Everyone ...........................................................................47
She Will Heal Us ..............................................................................48
Sister Spirit Shows the Healing Way ................................................50
Spirit of Life and Love ......................................................................55
Spirit of Love .....................................................................................56
The Spirit of Life ...............................................................................59
We Are Rising Up Together .............................................................64
We Celebrate Her Many Names ......................................................65
We Will Unite ...................................................................................68
We're Not Alone ...............................................................................69
When We Are Struggling with Doubt and Fear ..............................70
Who Will Bring Relief? ....................................................................72
Wisdom Sophia Is Calling ................................................................73

**HOPE**

Christ-Sophia, Give Us Wisdom .......................................................1
Come, Give Us Power for Our Day ...................................................6
Gather Everywhere in Circles ..........................................................16
Hokmah Wisdom Shows the Way ...................................................20
Holy Wisdom Fills Our Hearts with Song .......................................22
Join to Create ....................................................................................26
Keeping Hope Alive .........................................................................27
Liberating Christ-Sophia ..................................................................28
On Our Journey ................................................................................38
Our Loving Mother ..........................................................................40
Our Mother Inspires All Our Work .................................................39
Spirit of Life and Love ......................................................................55

Spirit of Love ..................................................................................................... 56
Spirit of Power ................................................................................................... 57
The Power of Love ............................................................................................ 58
They Who Wait .................................................................................................. 61
We're Not Alone ................................................................................................ 69
When We Are Struggling with Doubt and Fear ........................................... 70
Wisdom Sophia Is Calling ................................................................................ 73
Wisdom Sophia Keeps Giving .......................................................................... 74

## LABOR

Come, Holy Spirit, Bring Your Vision ............................................................. 7
Come Now, All-Inclusive Spirit ....................................................................... 8
Great Is Sophia ................................................................................................. 17
In These Times of Deep Division ................................................................... 24
Our Loving Mother .......................................................................................... 40
Our Mother Inspires All Our Work ............................................................... 39
Our Sister Spirit ................................................................................................ 41
Power in Us All ................................................................................................. 43
She Calls Everyone ........................................................................................... 47
Shekhinah Is Shining on Earth ....................................................................... 49
Sister Spirit Shows the Healing Way .............................................................. 50
Spirit of Power .................................................................................................. 57
There's Justice Work for Us to Do .................................................................. 60
We Are Dreaming of a World ......................................................................... 63
We Will Unite ................................................................................................... 68

## LIBERATION (see also Freedom)

Christ-Sophia, Give Us Wisdom ...................................................................... 1
Circles of Freedom ............................................................................................. 2
Come and Seek Sophia Wisdom ...................................................................... 4
Come, Give Us Power for Our Day ................................................................. 6
Come, Holy Spirit, Bring Your Vision ............................................................. 7
Come Quickly, Sophia ....................................................................................... 9
Come Together, Celebrate ..................................................................... 10, 10a
Creative Darkness Fills the Earth .................................................................. 11

Ever Embracing ∞ Ever Becoming ............................................................13
Every Moment the Divine Gives Life .......................................................14
Great Is Sophia .........................................................................................17
Hear Her Urgent Cry ...............................................................................19
Hokmah Wisdom Shows the Way ...........................................................20
Holy Wisdom Fills Our Hearts with Song................................................22
In These Times of Deep Division .............................................................24
Join All Together As One..........................................................................25
Join to Create............................................................................................26
Liberating Spirit Calls ...............................................................................29
Loving Shepherd Comes to Guide Us .....................................................31
Move Throughout Our World Today ......................................................33
New Life Awaits Us All .............................................................................34
Now Her Voice Liberates..........................................................................35
O Mother Godde ......................................................................................36
Our Sister Spirit.........................................................................................41
Ruah Spirit Calls Within...........................................................................45
She Calls Everyone ...................................................................................47
Sister Spirit Shows the Healing Way........................................................50
Sister-Brother Spirit Sets Us Free .............................................................51
So Many People Cry in Pain ....................................................................52
Spirit of Life and Love ..............................................................................55
Spirit of Love.............................................................................................56
Spirit of Power ..........................................................................................57
We Are Building on Her Love Eternal.....................................................62
We Are Dreaming of a World ..................................................................63
We Celebrate Her Many Names ..............................................................65
We Will Unite ...........................................................................................68
When We Are Struggling with Doubt and Fear .....................................70
Who Will Bring Relief?.............................................................................72
Wisdom Sophia Keeps Giving..................................................................74

## LOVE

Come, El Shaddai, with Tender Care.........................................................5
Come, Holy Spirit, Bring Your Vision........................................................7

| | |
|---|---|
| Come Now, All-Inclusive Spirit | 8 |
| Come Together, Celebrate | 10, 10a |
| El Shaddai | 12 |
| Ever Embracing ∞ Ever Becoming | 13 |
| Every Moment the Divine Gives Life | 14 |
| Friend of All | 15 |
| Hear Her Urgent Cry | 19 |
| Holy Wisdom Fills Our Hearts with Song | 22 |
| In These Times of Deep Division | 24 |
| Join All Together As One | 25 |
| Join to Create | 26 |
| Longing for Healing Peace | 30 |
| Loving Shepherd Calls | 32 |
| Move Throughout Our World Today | 33 |
| O Mother Godde, I Come | 37 |
| On Our Journey | 38 |
| Our Loving Mother | 40 |
| Our Mother Inspires All Our Work | 39 |
| Pillar of Salt | 42 |
| Ruah Spirit Calls Within | 45 |
| She Will Heal Us | 48 |
| Shekhinah Is Shining on Earth | 49 |
| Sister Spirit Shows the Healing Way | 50 |
| Sister-Brother Spirit Sets Us Free | 51 |
| So Many People Cry in Pain | 52 |
| Spirit of Life and Love | 55 |
| Spirit of Love | 56 |
| The Power of Love | 58 |
| We Are Building on Her Love Eternal | 62 |
| We Are Dreaming of a World | 63 |
| We Are Rising Up Together | 64 |
| We Must Follow Her Way | 67 |
| When We Rise Up All Together | 71 |

**MIRACLE**

Come Together, Celebrate .................................................................. 10, 10a
Creative Darkness Fills the Earth ................................................................ 11
In Her Power We Are Rising ....................................................................... 23
Sacred Darkness, Deep Within Us .............................................................. 46
She Will Heal Us ......................................................................................... 48
Sophia Wisdom Gives Us Power ................................................................. 53

**MISSION**

Come, Holy Spirit, Bring Your Vision ........................................................... 7
Come Now, All-Inclusive Spirit ..................................................................... 8
Join All Together As One ............................................................................. 25
On Our Journey ........................................................................................... 38
Pillar of Salt ................................................................................................. 42
We Will Unite ............................................................................................... 68
Who Will Bring Relief? ................................................................................. 72

**NEW LIFE**

Come and See a Revelation ......................................................................... 3
Come, Give Us Power for Our Day ............................................................... 6
Come, Holy Spirit, Bring Your Vision ........................................................... 7
Come Together, Celebrate .................................................................. 10, 10a
Creative Darkness Fills the Earth ................................................................ 11
Every Moment the Divine Gives Life .......................................................... 14
Friend of All ................................................................................................. 15
Hear Her Urgent Cry ................................................................................... 19
Holy Wisdom Calls ...................................................................................... 21
In These Times of Deep Division ................................................................ 24
Liberating Christ-Sophia ............................................................................. 28
New Life Awaits Us All ................................................................................ 34
Our Loving Mother ...................................................................................... 40
Power in Us All ............................................................................................ 43
Ruah Spirit Calls Within .............................................................................. 45
Sacred Darkness, Deep Within Us .............................................................. 46

Shekhinah Is Shining on Earth................................................................49
So Many People Cry in Pain ..................................................................52
Sophia Wisdom Gives Us Power............................................................53
Spirit of Godde, Spark of Creation.........................................................54
Spirit of Life and Love ............................................................................55
Spirit of Love...........................................................................................56
Spirit of Power ........................................................................................57
The Power of Love ..................................................................................58
The Spirit of Life.....................................................................................59
We Are Building on Her Love Eternal...................................................62
We Searched Many Years for a Spiritual Home ...................................66
When We Are Struggling with Doubt and Fear ...................................70
Wisdom Sophia Is Calling......................................................................73

## PARTNERSHIP

Circles of Freedom....................................................................................2
Come, Give Us Power for Our Day.........................................................6
Holy Wisdom Fills Our Hearts with Song............................................22
In These Times of Deep Division ..........................................................24
Join All Together Now ...........................................................................25
Join to Create..........................................................................................26
Keeping Hope Alive................................................................................27
New Life Awaits Us All ..........................................................................34
Rise Up Together Now ...........................................................................44
Ruah Spirit Calls Within........................................................................45
She Calls Everyone .................................................................................47
Shekhinah Is Shining on Earth..............................................................49
Sister-Brother Spirit Sets Us Free .........................................................51
Spirit of Power ........................................................................................57
We Are Dreaming of a World................................................................63
We Are Rising Up Together ..................................................................64
We Searched Many Years for a Spiritual Home ...................................66
We Will Unite.........................................................................................68
When We Rise Up All Together ............................................................71
Who Will Bring Relief?..........................................................................72

## PEACE

| | |
|---|---|
| Christ-Sophia, Give Us Wisdom | 1 |
| Circles of Freedom | 2 |
| Come and See a Revelation | 3 |
| Come and Seek Sophia Wisdom | 4 |
| Come, El Shaddai, with Tender Care | 5 |
| Come, Give Us Power for Our Day | 6 |
| Come, Holy Spirit, Bring Your Vision | 7 |
| Come Now, All-Inclusive Spirit | 8 |
| Come Quickly, Sophia | 9 |
| Gather Everywhere in Circles | 16 |
| Great Is Sophia | 17 |
| Hear Her Urgent Cry | 19 |
| Holy Wisdom Calls | 21 |
| Holy Wisdom Fills Our Hearts with Song | 22 |
| In These Times of Deep Division | 24 |
| Join All Together As One | 25 |
| Join to Create | 26 |
| Liberating Christ-Sophia | 28 |
| Liberating Spirit Calls | 29 |
| Longing for Healing Peace | 30 |
| Loving Shepherd Comes to Guide Us | 31 |
| Move Throughout Our World Today | 33 |
| Now Her Voice Liberates | 35 |
| O Mother Godde | 36 |
| On Our Journey | 38 |
| Our Loving Mother | 40 |
| Our Mother Inspires All Our Work | 39 |
| Our Sister Spirit | 41 |
| Power in Us All | 43 |
| Rise Up Together Now | 44 |
| Ruah Spirit Calls Within | 45 |
| Sacred Darkness, Deep Within Us | 46 |
| She Calls Everyone | 47 |
| Shekhinah Is Shining on Earth | 49 |
| Sister Spirit Shows the Healing Way | 50 |

Sister-Brother Spirit Sets Us Free ..............................................................................51
So Many People Cry in Pain ..........................................................................................52
Sophia Wisdom Gives Us Power ...................................................................................53
Spirit of Love ....................................................................................................................56
Spirit of Power .................................................................................................................57
The Power of Love ...........................................................................................................58
The Spirit of Life ..............................................................................................................59
There's Justice Work for Us to Do ................................................................................60
They Who Wait ................................................................................................................61
We Are Building on Her Love Eternal .........................................................................62
We Celebrate Her Many Names ....................................................................................65
When We Are Struggling with Doubt and Fear .........................................................70
When We Rise Up All Together ....................................................................................71
Wisdom Sophia Keeps Giving .......................................................................................74

## PENTECOST

Come, Holy Spirit, Bring Your Vision ............................................................................7
Come Now, All-Inclusive Spirit .......................................................................................8
Join All Together As One ................................................................................................25
Liberating Spirit Calls .....................................................................................................29
Move Throughout Our World Today ..........................................................................33
New Life Awaits Us All ...................................................................................................34
Ruah Spirit Calls Within ................................................................................................45
Sister-Brother Spirit Sets Us Free ..................................................................................51
Spirit of Godde, Spark of Creation ...............................................................................54
Spirit of Life and Love ....................................................................................................55
Spirit of Love ....................................................................................................................56
Spirit of Power .................................................................................................................57
The Spirit of Life ..............................................................................................................59
We Will Unite ..................................................................................................................68

## POWER

Christ-Sophia, Give Us Wisdom .....................................................................................1
Circles of Freedom ............................................................................................................2
Come and Seek Sophia Wisdom .....................................................................................4

| | |
|---|---|
| Come, Give Us Power for Our Day | 6 |
| Come, Holy Spirit, Bring Your Vision | 7 |
| Come Quickly, Sophia | 9 |
| Come Together, Celebrate | 10, 10a |
| Creative Darkness Fills the Earth | 11 |
| El Shaddai | 12 |
| Every Moment the Divine Gives Life | 14 |
| Friend of All | 15 |
| Gather Everywhere in Circles | 16 |
| Great Is Sophia | 17 |
| Guiding on Healing Paths | 18 |
| Hokmah Wisdom Shows the Way | 20 |
| Holy Wisdom Fills Our Hearts with Song | 22 |
| In Her Power We Are Rising | 23 |
| In These Times of Deep Division | 24 |
| Join All Together As One | 25 |
| Liberating Christ-Sophia | 28 |
| Liberating Spirit Calls | 29 |
| Loving Shepherd Comes to Guide Us | 31 |
| Move Throughout Our World Today | 33 |
| New Life Awaits Us All | 34 |
| Our Loving Mother | 40 |
| Our Mother Inspires All Our Work | 39 |
| Pillar of Salt | 42 |
| Power in Us All | 43 |
| Rise Up Together Now | 44 |
| Sacred Darkness, Deep Within Us | 46 |
| Sister Spirit Shows the Healing Way | 50 |
| Sister-Brother Spirit Sets Us Free | 51 |
| So Many People Cry in Pain | 52 |
| Sophia Wisdom Gives Us Power | 53 |
| Spirit of Godde, Spark of Creation | 54 |
| Spirit of Life and Love | 55 |
| Spirit of Love | 56 |
| Spirit of Power | 57 |
| The Spirit of Life | 59 |
| There's Justice Work for Us to Do | 60 |

They Who Wait ................................................................................................... 61
We Are Building on Her Love Eternal ................................................................. 62
We Celebrate Her Many Names ........................................................................... 65
We Searched Many Years for a Spiritual Home ................................................. 66
We Will Unite ....................................................................................................... 68
When We Are Struggling with Doubt and Fear ................................................. 70
When We Rise Up All Together .......................................................................... 71
Wisdom Sophia Is Calling ................................................................................... 73
Wisdom Sophia Keeps Giving ............................................................................. 74

## PRAISE (see also Thanksgiving)

Come, Give Us Power for Our Day ....................................................................... 6
Come Together, Celebrate ........................................................................... 10, 10a
El Shaddai ............................................................................................................. 12
Ever Embracing ∞ Ever Becoming ..................................................................... 13
O Mother Godde .................................................................................................. 36
Sophia Wisdom Gives Us Power ......................................................................... 53
We Celebrate Her Many Names ........................................................................... 65
We Must Follow Her Way .................................................................................... 67

## RENEWAL

Come, Holy Spirit, Bring Your Vision .................................................................. 7
Creative Darkness Fills the Earth ........................................................................ 11
Every Moment the Divine Gives Life ................................................................. 14
Great Is Sophia ..................................................................................................... 17
In Her Power We Are Rising ............................................................................... 23
Liberating Christ-Sophia ..................................................................................... 28
Longing for Healing Peace .................................................................................. 30
Loving Shepherd Calls ......................................................................................... 32
Loving Shepherd Comes to Guide Us ................................................................. 31
Move Throughout Our World Today ................................................................. 33
New Life Awaits Us All ........................................................................................ 34
O Mother Godde .................................................................................................. 36
O Mother Godde, I Come .................................................................................... 37
Our Loving Mother ............................................................................................. 40
Our Mother Inspires All Our Work .................................................................... 39

She Will Heal Us .................................................................................................48
Spirit of Godde, Spark of Creation......................................................................54
The Spirit of Life..................................................................................................59
There's Justice Work for Us to Do.......................................................................60
They Who Wait ....................................................................................................61
We Celebrate Her Many Names ..........................................................................65
We Searched Many Years for a Spiritual Home .................................................66
We're Not Alone ...................................................................................................69
When We Rise Up All Together ..........................................................................71

## RESURRECTION

Come and See a Revelation ..................................................................................3
Move Throughout Our World Today .................................................................33
Rise Up Together Now ........................................................................................44
Shekhinah Is Shining on Earth ...........................................................................49
When We Rise Up All Together ..........................................................................71

## SOCIAL JUSTICE

Christ-Sophia, Give Us Wisdom...........................................................................1
Come and Seek Sophia Wisdom...........................................................................4
Come, Holy Spirit, Bring Your Vision..................................................................7
Come Together, Celebrate .......................................................................... 10, 10a
Creative Darkness Fills the Earth.......................................................................11
Friend of All.........................................................................................................15
Great Is Sophia ....................................................................................................17
Hear Her Urgent Cry ..........................................................................................19
Hokmah Wisdom Shows the Way ......................................................................20
Holy Wisdom Calls .............................................................................................21
In These Times of Deep Division.......................................................................24
Join to Create.......................................................................................................26
Liberating Spirit Calls ........................................................................................29
Longing for Healing Peace .................................................................................30
Move Throughout Our World Today .................................................................33
New Life Awaits Us All .......................................................................................34
Now Her Voice Liberates....................................................................................35

On Our Journey ..................................................................................................38
Our Mother Inspires All Our Work..................................................................39
Our Sister Spirit..................................................................................................41
Pillar of Salt........................................................................................................42
Power in Us All...................................................................................................43
Rise Up Together Now .......................................................................................44
Ruah Spirit Calls Within....................................................................................45
Sacred Darkness, Deep Within Us.....................................................................46
She Calls Everyone .............................................................................................47
She Will Heal Us ................................................................................................48
Shekhinah Is Shining on Earth..........................................................................49
Sister Spirit Shows the Healing Way .................................................................50
Sister-Brother Spirit Sets Us Free ......................................................................51
Spirit of Life and Love .......................................................................................55
Spirit of Love......................................................................................................56
Spirit of Power....................................................................................................57
The Power of Love .............................................................................................58
The Spirit of Life................................................................................................59
There's Justice Work for Us to Do.....................................................................60
We Are Building on Her Love Eternal...............................................................62
We Are Dreaming of a World ............................................................................63
We Are Rising Up Together ...............................................................................64
We Celebrate Her Many Names ........................................................................65
We Must Follow Her Way..................................................................................67
We Searched Many Years for a Spiritual Home ................................................66
We Will Unite.....................................................................................................68
When We Are Struggling with Doubt and Fear ................................................70
When We Rise Up All Together .........................................................................71
Who Will Bring Relief?......................................................................................72
Wisdom Sophia Keeps Giving............................................................................74

## THANKSGIVING (see also Praise)

Come, Give Us Power for Our Day.....................................................................6
Come Together, Celebrate ........................................................................ 10, 10a
El Shaddai..........................................................................................................12
Ever Embracing ∞ Ever Becoming ....................................................................13

O Mother Godde .................................................................................................36
Sophia Wisdom Gives Us Power .......................................................................53
We Celebrate Her Many Names ........................................................................65
We Must Follow Her Way..................................................................................67

**TRANSFORMATION**

Circles of Freedom..............................................................................................2
Come and See a Revelation ................................................................................3
Come, Holy Spirit, Bring Your Vision ...............................................................7
Come Quickly, Sophia ........................................................................................9
Come Together, Celebrate ......................................................................... 10, 10a
Ever Embracing ∞ Ever Becoming ..................................................................13
Gather Everywhere in Circles ..........................................................................16
In These Times of Deep Division .....................................................................24
Move Throughout Our World Today ...............................................................33
O Mother Godde ...............................................................................................36
On Our Journey .................................................................................................38
Pillar of Salt........................................................................................................42
Ruah Spirit Calls Within...................................................................................45
Sister-Brother Spirit Sets Us Free ....................................................................51
Sophia Wisdom Gives Us Power ......................................................................53
Spirit of Life and Love ......................................................................................55
Spirit of Love......................................................................................................56
The Power of Love ............................................................................................58
We Are Building on Her Love Eternal.............................................................62
We Are Dreaming of a World ...........................................................................63
We Are Rising Up Together .............................................................................64
We Celebrate Her Many Names .......................................................................65
We Must Follow Her Way.................................................................................67
When We Are Struggling with Doubt and Fear .............................................70
When We Rise Up All Together .......................................................................71

**TRUTH**

Come and See a Revelation ................................................................................3
Come Quickly, Sophia ........................................................................................9
Holy Wisdom Calls ...........................................................................................21

Join to Create .......... 26
Longing for Healing Peace .......... 30
Our Sister Spirit .......... 41
Spirit of Love .......... 56
We Celebrate Her Many Names .......... 65
When We Are Struggling with Doubt and Fear .......... 70

## UNITY AND DIVERSITY

Come and See a Revelation .......... 3
Great Is Sophia .......... 17
Move Throughout Our World Today .......... 33
Sacred Darkness, Deep Within Us .......... 46
Sister-Brother Spirit Sets Us Free .......... 51

## VISION

Circles of Freedom .......... 2
Come and See a Revelation .......... 3
Come, Holy Spirit, Bring Your Vision .......... 7
Come Together, Celebrate .......... 10, 10a
Creative Darkness Fills the Earth .......... 11
Gather Everywhere in Circles .......... 16
Join to Create .......... 26
New Life Awaits Us All .......... 34
Now Her Voice Liberates .......... 35
On Our Journey .......... 38
Our Mother Inspires All Our Work .......... 39
Power in Us All .......... 43
Spirit of Godde, Spark of Creation .......... 54
Spirit of Power .......... 57
There's Justice Work for Us to Do .......... 60
We Are Building on Her Love Eternal .......... 62
We Are Dreaming of a World .......... 63
When We Are Struggling with Doubt and Fear .......... 70
When We Rise Up All Together .......... 71
Who Will Bring Relief? .......... 72

**WHOLENESS**

Great Is Sophia .................................................................................................17
Loving Shepherd Comes to Guide Us ...............................................................31
On Our Journey ................................................................................................38
Rise Up Together Now ......................................................................................44
She Calls Everyone ............................................................................................47
Spirit of Love.....................................................................................................56
We Are Building on Her Love Eternal...............................................................62

# INDEX OF SCRIPTURE REFERENCES

## Genesis

1 ................................................ 33, 55, 59
1:1-2 ........................................... 45, 65, 70
1:20-27 ................................................ 14
19:1-26 ................................................ 42
49:25 ........................................... 5, 12, 65

## Exodus

1:15-22 ................................................ 20
29:45 .............................................. 18, 65
40:34-38 ....................................... 18, 49, 65

## Deuteronomy

32:11-12 ....................................... 23, 39, 71
32:18 .................................................. 40

## Psalms

23 ..................................................... 31

## Proverbs

1:7 ................................................ 52, 58
1:20-21 ............................................ 47, 73
1:20-23 ... 19, 21, 24, 30, 35, 41, 52, 58, 65, 66
3:13-17 ................................................. 4
3:13-18 ...................... 21, 22, 43, 53, 65, 74
3:16-18 ................................................ 73
3:17 ......................... 1, 17, 19, 30, 52, 58
3:17-18 ........................... 6, 9, 24, 35, 47
4:8-9 .................................................. 53

## Isaiah

40:31 .................................................. 61
43:1-2 .................................................. 5
45:3 ............................................ 11, 41, 46
49:15 .............................................. 12, 39
61:1 ................................................... 72
66:13 ....................................... 12, 27, 40, 65

## Amos

5:22-24 ................................................ 21
5:24 ............................................. 19, 43, 68

## Micah

6:4 .................................................... 20
6:8 ................................................ 24, 74

## Matthew

3:16 ................................................ 29, 48
25:35-40 ............................................... 41

## Luke

4:18 ......................................... 9, 17, 28, 72
15:3-7 ................................................. 32
24:1-12 ................................................. 3

## John

4:7-42 .................................................. 3
8:32 ........................................... 2, 34, 32, 57
14:17 .................................................. 70
15:15 .............................................. 15, 65
20:11-18 ................................................ 3

## Acts

1:8 .................................................. 25
2:1-17 ............................................ 33
2:17 ........................................ 34, 66

## Romans

8:2 .................................................. 55
8:18-25 ............................................ 7
8:22-27 .......................................... 56
8:24-25 .......................................... 27
8:26 ................................................ 38
8:26-27 .......................................... 48
15:13 .............................................. 25

## 1 Corinthians

1:24 ...................... 1, 4, 6, 9, 17, 28, 65
12:4-11 ...................................... 8, 50

## 2 Corinthians

3:17 ............................................ 2, 51
5:17 ................................................ 45

## Galatians

5:22 ............... 2, 7, 8, 16, 38, 45, 51, 56, 63

## Ephesians

4:3-4 .............................................. 68

## Philippians

1:3-5 ........................................ 10, 10a

## Colossians

3:16 .......................................... 10, 10a

## 2 Timothy

1:7 ................................ 29, 44, 57, 59

## 1 John

4:18 ................................................ 58

# INDEX OF COMPOSERS, AUTHORS, AND SOURCES

Alwood, J. K. (1828-1909) ............................................................................................... 63
American folk hymn ......................................................................................................... 1
American folk melody .................................................................................................... 41
American folk song ........................................................................................................ 25
American melody ............................................................................................................. 9
Beethoven, Ludwig van (1770-1827) ............................................................................. 10
Bennard, George (1873-1960) ....................................................................................... 58
Bilhorn, P. P. (1865-1936) .............................................................................................. 23
Black, James M. (1856-1938) ........................................................................................ 71
Bradbury, William B. (1816-1868) ................................................................................. 37
Brahms, Johannes (1833-1897) ..................................................................................... 17
Bridgers, Luther B. (1884-1948) .............................................................................. 22, 29
Brown, McKenzie (1993- ) ............................................... 26, 36, 37, 60, 62, 64, 67, 69
Brumley, Albert E. (1905-1977) .................................................................................... 34
Bushey, J. Calvin (1847-1929) ....................................................................................... 47
Calvisius, Seth (1556-1615) ........................................................................................... 20
Cook, George Harrison (1859-1933) ............................................................................ 57
Croft, William (1678-1727) ........................................................................................ 6, 59
Decius, Nicolaus (1485-1546) ........................................................................................ 65
Early American melody .................................................................................................. 52
Ellor, James (1819-1899) ............................................................................................... 53
*Enchiridia*, Erfurt (1524) ................................................................................................ 20
Entwisle, J. Howard (1865-1901) .................................................................................. 44
Fillmore, James H. (1849-1936) .................................................................................... 68
Gabriel, Charles H. (1856-1932) .............................................................................. 27, 64
Grape, John T. (1835-1915) ........................................................................................... 32
Graves, F. A. (1856-1927) .............................................................................................. 60
Grétry, A. (1741-1813) ................................................................................................... 40
Hays, William S. (1837-1907) ....................................................................................... 31
Hérold, Ferdinand (1791-1833) ..................................................................................... 33
Hoffman, E. A. (1839-1929) .......................................................................................... 35
Hugg, George C. (1848-1907) ....................................................................................... 15

Isaiah 40:31 .................................................................................................................. 61
Jones, Lewis E. (1865-1936) ........................................................................... 43
Kirkpatrick, William J. (1838-1921) ............................................................ 8, 19, 39
Leavitt, Joshua (1794-1873) ............................................................................. 3
Lowry, Robert (1826-1899) ....................................................................... 16, 28
McAfee, Cleland Boyd (1866-1944) ............................................................... 18
McGranahan, James (1840-1907) ................................................................. 73
McKinney, B. B. (1886-1952) ......................................................................... 50
Moody, Charles E. (1891-1977) ................................................................ 26, 30
Moore, George D. (1800-1900) ..................................................................... 66
Norris, John S. (1844-1907) ............................................................................. 4
Norwegian folk melody .................................................................................. 40
Parry, C. Hubert H. (1848-1918) .................................................................... 11
Pitts, William S. (1829-1903) ........................................................................... 2
Plainsong melody ..................................................................................... 24, 45
Scholefield, Clement C. (1839-1904) .............................................................. 7
Schultz, Larry E. (1965- ) ............................. 10a, 13, 17, 24, 25, 41, 42, 45, 46, 54, 55, 61, 72
Sellers, Earnest O. (1869-1952) ..................................................................... 74
Stebbins, George C. (1846-1945) ................................................................... 56
Stevens, W. B. (1862-ca.1940) ....................................................................... 69
Stockton, John H. (1813-1877) ................................................................. 21, 48
*Supplement to the Kentucky Harmony* (Ananias Davisson, 1820) .................. 46
Swedish folk melody ...................................................................................... 36
Swedish folk tune .......................................................................................... 55
Sweney, John R. (1837-1869) ........................................................................ 49
Tindley, Charles Albert (1851-1933) ......................................................... 12, 50
Tomer, William G. (1833-1896) ..................................................................... 14
Towner, Daniel B. (1850-1919) ................................................................. 51, 70
Warren, Barney Elliott (1867-1951) ............................................................. 62
Webster, Joseph Philbrick (1819-1875) ........................................................ 67
Wilson, Hugh (1764-1824) .............................................................................. 5
Wright, J. B. F. (1877-1959) .......................................................................... 38

# ALPHABETICAL INDEX OF TUNES

ADORO TE DEVOTE, 12.12.13.13................................................................45
ALL TO CHRIST, Irregular with refrain.......................................................32
ALLEIN GOTT IN DER HÖH, 8.7.8.7.8.8.7..................................................65
ARE YOU BUILDING ON THE ROCK ETERNAL, 10.9.10.9 with refrain........62
BY AND BY, 7.7.8.7.7.7.11 with refrain.......................................................50
CALVARY, 9.9.9.4 with refrain...................................................................51
CALVIN, 8.8.8.5 with refrain.....................................................................47
CLEANSING FOUNTAIN, 8.6.8.6.6.6.8.6....................................................52
COME AND ARISE, Irregular.....................................................................72
COMING HOME, 8.5.8.5 with refrain.........................................................19
CRISP, 12.12.12.10.11...............................................................................42
DIADEM, 8.6.6.8 with refrain....................................................................53
DIVINUM MYSTERIUM, 8.7.8.7.8.7.7........................................................24
DOWN TO THE RIVER, 10.9.8.6 with refrain.............................................25
FARTHER ALONG, 10.9.10.9 with refrain..................................................69
FAYETTEVILLE STREET, 10.10.10.10..........................................................13
GLORY TO HIS NAME, 9.9.9.5 with refrain................................................21
GOD BE WITH YOU, 9.8.8.9 with refrain...................................................14
HANOVER, 10.10.11.11..............................................................................59
HANSON PLACE, 8.7.8.7 with refrain........................................................16
HARPER MEMORIAL, 10.6.10.6 with refrain.............................................15
HAVEN OF REST, 11.8.12.8 with refrain....................................................66
HIGHER GROUND, 8.8.8.8 (LM) with refrain.............................................27
HYMN TO JOY, 8.7.8.7 D............................................................................10
JESUS, I COME, 9.8.9.6.9.9.9.6..................................................................56
JUBILEE, alt., 8.7.8.7 D..............................................................................46
KIRKPATRICK, 11.8.11.8 with refrain........................................................39
KNEEL AT THE CROSS, 9.6.9.6 with refrain..............................................26
LAND OF REST, 8.6.8.6 (CM).....................................................................41
LANDÅS, 8.6.8.6 (CM) with refrain...........................................................40
LONESOME VALLEY, 8.8.10.8.....................................................................1
MARTYRDOM (also AVON), 8.6.8.6 (CM)....................................................5
McAFEE, 8.6.8.6 (CM) with refrain............................................................18
MESSIAH, 7.7.7.7 D...................................................................................33
MOODY, 9.9.9.9 with refrain.....................................................................70
NEW ORLEANS, 9.8.9.6 with refrain..........................................................74
NORRIS, 8.8.8.9 with refrain.......................................................................4

| Tune | Meter | Page |
|---|---|---|
| NUN KOMM DER HEIDEN HEILAND | 7.7.7.7 | 20 |
| O HOW I LOVE JESUS | 8.6.8.6 (CM) with refrain | 9 |
| O MY BROTHER, DO YOU KNOW THE SAVIOR | 10.7.8.8 with refrain | 60 |
| O STORE GUD | 11.10.11.10 with refrain | 36 |
| OLD RUGGED CROSS | 12.8.12.8 with refrain | 58 |
| OUT ON THE PERILOUS DEEP | 7.7.7.8 with refrain | 30 |
| PLAINFIELD | 7.8.7.8 with refrain | 28 |
| PLEADING SAVIOR | 8.7.8.7 D | 3 |
| POWER IN THE BLOOD | 10.9.10.8 with refrain | 43 |
| PRECIOUS MEM'RIES, UNSEEN ANGELS | 8.7.8.7 with refrain | 38 |
| RENEWAL | Irregular | 54 |
| REPTON | 8.6.8.8.6.6 | 11 |
| RESOLUTION | 10.6.10.6 with refrain | 68 |
| ROLL CALL | 15.11.15.11 with refrain | 71 |
| SALVATIONIST | Irregular with refrain | 31 |
| SHOWERS OF BLESSING | 8.7.8.7 with refrain | 73 |
| SPIRIT DANCE | 8.7.8.7 D | 10a |
| ST. ANNE | 8.6.8.6 (CM) | 6 |
| ST. CLEMENT | 9.8.9.8 | 7 |
| STAND BY ME | 8.3.8.3.7.7.8.3 | 12 |
| STARS IN MY CROWN | 12.9.12.9 with refrain | 49 |
| STOCKTON | 8.6.8.6 (CM) with refrain | 48 |
| SUNLIGHT | 10.9.10.9 with refrain | 57 |
| SWEET BY AND BY | 9.9.9.9 with refrain | 67 |
| SWEETEST NAME | 9.7.9.7 with refrain | 22, 29 |
| SYMPHONY | 12.12.8.6.8.9 | 17 |
| THE UNCLOUDED DAY | 12.10.12.10 with refrain | 63 |
| THIS WORLD IS NOT MY HOME | 12.12.12.12 with refrain | 34 |
| TROUBLED SIDE OF LIFE | 10.9.9.9 with refrain | 44 |
| TRUST IN JESUS | 8.7.8.7 with refrain | 8 |
| UNBROKEN CIRCLE | 8.7.8.7 with refrain | 64 |
| VÅRVINDAR FRISKA | 11.6.11.5 with refrain | 55 |
| WAIT | 6.10.6.10 | 61 |
| WASHED IN THE BLOOD | 11.9.11.9 with refrain | 35 |
| WILDWOOD | 11.8.9.9 with refrain | 2 |
| WONDROUS STORY | 8.7.8.7 with refrain | 23 |
| WOODWORTH | 8.8.8.8 (LM) | 37 |

# METRICAL INDEX OF TUNES

**6.10.6.10**
WAIT ..................................................61

**7.7.7.7**
NUN KOMM DER HEIDEN HEILAND...20

**7.7.7.7 D**
MESSIAH ..........................................33

**7.7.7.8 with refrain**
OUT ON THE PERILOUS DEEP ..........30

**7.7.8.7.7.7.11 with refrain**
BY AND BY......................................50

**7.8.7.8 with refrain**
PLAINFIELD ....................................28

**8.3.8.3.7.7.8.3**
STAND BY ME..................................12

**8.5.8.5 with refrain**
COMING HOME................................19

**8.6.6.8 with refrain**
DIADEM...........................................53

**8.6.8.6 (CM)**
LAND OF REST................................41
MARTYRDOM (also AVON ..................5
ST. ANNE .........................................6

**8.6.8.6 (CM) with refrain**
LANDÅS...........................................40
McAFEE...........................................18
O HOW I LOVE JESUS........................9
STOCKTON.......................................48

**8.6.8.6.6.6.8.6**
CLEANSING FOUNTAIN ..................52

**8.6.8.8.6.6**
REPTON ..........................................11

**8.7.8.7 with refrain**
HANSON PLACE...............................16
PRECIOUS MEM'RIES,
UNSEEN ANGELS ............................38
SHOWERS OF BLESSING..................73
TRUST IN JESUS ...............................8
UNBROKEN CIRCLE.........................64
WONDROUS STORY ........................23

**8.7.8.7 D**
HYMN TO JOY ................................10
JUBILEE, alt....................................46
PLEADING SAVIOR............................3
SPIRIT DANCE................................10a

**8.7.8.7.8.7.7**
DIVINUM MYSTERIUM...................24

**8.7.8.7.8.8.7**
ALLEIN GOTT IN DER HÖH..........65

**8.8.8.5 with refrain**
CALVIN...........................................47
PLAINFIELD....................................28

**8.8.8.8 (LM)**
WOODWORTH ...................................... 37

**8.8.8.8 (LM) with refrain**
HIGHER GROUND ............................. 27

**8.8.8.9 with refrain**
NORRIS ...................................................... 4

**8.8.10.8**
LONESOME VALLEY ............................ 1

**9.6.9.6 with refrain**
KNEEL AT THE CROSS ...................... 26

**9.7.9.7 with refrain**
SWEETEST NAME ........................ 22, 29

**9.8.8.9 with refrain**
GOD BE WITH YOU ........................... 14

**9.8.9.6 with refrain**
NEW ORLEANS .................................... 74

**9.8.9.6.9.9.9.6**
JESUS, I COME ..................................... 56

**9.8.9.8**
ST. CLEMENT ........................................ 7

**9.9.9.4 with refrain**
CALVARY ............................................... 51

**9.9.9.5 with refrain**
GLORY TO HIS NAME ...................... 21

**9.9.9.9 with refrain**
MOODY .................................................. 70
SWEET BY AND BY ............................ 67

**10.6.10.6 with refrain**
HARPER MEMORIAL ......................... 15
RESOLUTION ....................................... 68

**10.7.8.8 with refrain**
O MY BROTHER, DO YOU
KNOW THE SAVIOR .......................... 60

**10.9.8.6 with refrain**
DOWN TO THE RIVER ..................... 25

**10.9.9.9 with refrain**
TROUBLED SIDE OF LIFE ............... 44

**10.9.10.8 with refrain**
POWER IN THE BLOOD ................... 43

**10.9.10.9 with refrain**
ARE YOU BUILDING
ON THE ROCK ETERNAL ................ 62
FARTHER ALONG ............................... 69
SUNLIGHT ............................................ 57

**10.10.10.10**
FAYETTEVILLE STREET .................... 13

**10.10.11.11**
HANOVER .............................................. 59

**11.6.11.5 with refrain**
VÅRVINDAR FRISKA ......................... 55

**11.8.9.9 with refrain**
WILDWOOD .................................................. 2

**11.8.11.8 with refrain**
KIRKPATRICK ............................................ 39

**11.8.12.8 with refrain**
HAVEN OF REST ....................................... 66

**11.9.11.9 with refrain**
WASHED IN THE BLOOD ................ 35

**11.10.11.10 with refrain**
O STORE GUD ........................................... 36

**12.8.12.8 with refrain**
OLD RUGGED CROSS .......................... 58

**12.9.12.9 with refrain**
STARS IN MY CROWN ....................... 49

**12.10.12.10 with refrain**
THE UNCLOUDED DAY .................... 63

**12.12.8.6.8.9**
SYMPHONY ............................................... 17

**12.12.12.10.11**
CRISP ............................................................... 42

**12.12.12.12 with refrain**
THIS WORLD IS NOT MY HOME .. 34

**12.12.13.13**
ADORO TE DEVOTE ............................ 45

**15.11.15.11 with refrain**
ROLL CALL ................................................. 71

**Irregular**
COME AND ARISE ................................ 72
RENEWAL .................................................. 54

**Irregular with refrain**
ALL TO CHRIST ...................................... 32
SALVATIONIST ....................................... 31

# INDEX OF TITLES

| | |
|---|---|
| Christ-Sophia, Give Us Wisdom | 1 |
| Circles of Freedom | 2 |
| Come and See a Revelation | 3 |
| Come and Seek Sophia Wisdom | 4 |
| Come, El Shaddai, with Tender Care | 5 |
| Come, Give Us Power for Our Day | 6 |
| Come, Holy Spirit, Bring Your Vision | 7 |
| Come Now, All-Inclusive Spirit | 8 |
| Come Quickly, Sophia | 9 |
| Come Together, Celebrate | 10, 10a |
| Creative Darkness Fills the Earth | 11 |
| El Shaddai | 12 |
| Ever Embracing ∞ Ever Becoming | 13 |
| Every Moment the Divine Gives Life | 14 |
| Friend of All | 15 |
| Gather Everywhere in Circles | 16 |
| Great Is Sophia | 17 |
| Guiding on Healing Paths | 18 |
| Hear Her Urgent Cry | 19 |
| Hokmah Wisdom Shows the Way | 20 |
| Holy Wisdom Calls | 21 |
| Holy Wisdom Fills Our Hearts with Song | 22 |
| In Her Power We Are Rising | 23 |
| In These Times of Deep Division | 24 |
| Join All Together As One | 25 |
| Join to Create | 26 |
| Keeping Hope Alive | 27 |
| Liberating Christ-Sophia | 28 |
| Liberating Spirit Calls | 29 |
| Longing for Healing Peace | 30 |
| Loving Shepherd Calls | 32 |
| Loving Shepherd Comes to Guide Us | 31 |
| Move Throughout Our World Today | 33 |
| New Life Awaits Us All | 34 |

| | |
|---|---|
| Now Her Voice Liberates | 35 |
| O Mother Godde | 36 |
| O Mother Godde, I Come | 37 |
| On Our Journey | 38 |
| Our Loving Mother | 40 |
| Our Mother Inspires All Our Work | 39 |
| Our Sister Spirit | 41 |
| Pillar of Salt | 42 |
| Power in Us All | 43 |
| Rise Up Together Now | 44 |
| Ruah Spirit Calls Within | 45 |
| Sacred Darkness, Deep Within Us | 46 |
| She Calls Everyone | 47 |
| She Will Heal Us | 48 |
| Shekhinah Is Shining on Earth | 49 |
| Sister Spirit Shows the Healing Way | 50 |
| Sister-Brother Spirit Sets Us Free | 51 |
| So Many People Cry in Pain | 52 |
| Sophia Wisdom Gives Us Power | 53 |
| Spirit of Godde, Spark of Creation | 54 |
| Spirit of Life and Love | 55 |
| Spirit of Love | 56 |
| Spirit of Power | 57 |
| The Power of Love | 58 |
| The Spirit of Life | 59 |
| There's Justice Work for Us to Do | 60 |
| They Who Wait | 61 |
| We Are Building on Her Love Eternal | 62 |
| We Are Dreaming of a World | 63 |
| We Are Rising Up Together | 64 |
| We Celebrate Her Many Names | 65 |
| We Must Follow Her Way | 67 |
| We Searched Many Years for a Spiritual Home | 66 |
| We Will Unite | 68 |
| We're Not Alone | 69 |
| When We Are Struggling with Doubt and Fear | 70 |
| When We Rise Up All Together | 71 |
| Who Will Bring Relief? | 72 |
| Wisdom Sophia Is Calling | 73 |
| Wisdom Sophia Keeps Giving | 74 |

# *Books From Jann Aldredge-Clanton & Eakin Press*

### Breaking Free: The Story of a Feminist Baptist Minister
Jann Aldredge-Clanton didn't start out as a reformer. When she was a pre-teen, she almost starved herself to death trying to fit into the culture's feminine mold. In high school she felt inadequate because she never won a beauty crown, even though she graduated at the top of her class. Slowly, she began waking up to her own voice, and became one of the first women ever to be ordained as a Baptist minister in the South.

### In Search of the Christ-Sophia: An Inclusive Christology for Liberating Christians
presents powerful biblical and theological support for a Divine Feminine image buried in Christianity. The popularity of The Da Vinci Code demonstrates the widespread hunger for the lost Sacred Feminine. This book resurrects Sophia (Wisdom) and connects Her to Jesus Christ.

## *Hymnals & Songbooks*

### Inclusive Hymns for Liberating Christians
These hymns will lift the heart, invigorate the mind, and enliven the spirit. The wide variety of biblical divine names and images in this hymnbook will contribute to belief in the sacredness of all people and all creation. Peace and justice flow from this belief.

### Inclusive Hymns for Liberation, Peace, and Justice
Words we sing in worship have great power to shape our beliefs and actions. This is the second collection of hymns by Jann Aldredge-Clanton with composer Larry E. Schultz. These hymns, like those in the first collection, will contribute to an expansive theology and an ethic of equality and justice in human relationships.

### Earth Transformed with Music! Inclusive Songs for Worship
Music has great power to touch the heart and change the world. Words we sing in worship shape our beliefs and actions. The inclusive songs in this collection will contribute to social justice, peace, equality, and expansive spiritual experience. This collection includes all new songs, most to widely-known tunes and some to new tunes.

### Inclusive Songs for Resistance & Social Action
Music empowers action for social change. Music stirs our spirits and embeds words in our memories. Words shape our values that drive our actions. Singing our beliefs in justice, peace, and equality will move us to transform our world. *Inclusive Songs for Resistance & Social Action* will contribute to gender, racial, economic, environmental, and other justice movements.

### Inclusive Songs from the Heart of Gospel
Music has great power to spread the good news of peace, justice, liberation, and abundant life for all people. This new song collection proclaims this good news with lyrics inclusive in gender and race and with themes of social justice and peacemaking. The title of this collection, *Inclusive Songs from the Heart* of Gospel, comes from our choice of gospel music tunes for most of our texts.

## Eakin Press
PO Box 331779 • Fort Worth, Texas 76163 • 817-344-7036
### www.EakinPress.com
*A Subsidiary of Wild Horse Media Group*

www.ingramcontent.com/pod-product-compliance
Lightning Source LLC
Chambersburg PA
CBHW080413170426
43194CB00015B/2800